MW01136843

THE
KNIFE
THROWER'S
ASSISTANT

THE
KNIFE
THROWER'S
ASSISTANT

*Memoirs of a
Human Target*

by

**Ronnie Claire
Edwards**

Foreword by Fannie Flagg

HAWK Publishing

Published in the United States by
HAWK Publishing Group.

HAWK and colophon are trademarks belonging
to the HAWK Publishing Group.

Book and cover design by Carl Brune

Printed in the United States of America.

Library of Congress Cataloging in Publication Data
Edwards, Ronnie Claire
The Knife-Thrower's Assistant/Ronnie Claire
Edwards–HAWK Publishing ed.
p.   cm.
ISBN 1-930709-16-1 (hard cover)
ISBN 1-930709-19-6 (soft cover)

1.Autobiography
2. Oklahoma
I. Title
[PS3563.I42145R4 2000]
813'.54   80-52413
CIP

HAWK Publishing web address: www.hawkpub.com

H987654321

TABLE OF CONTENTS

Lovingly dedicated to

Papa and Mama

Special thanks to
Tom Foral
Edward Swift
Elizabeth Forsythe Hailey
(For putting up with me!)

Acknowledgement

I am thankful and appreciative to the following people for their generosity and support, but most of all, for their friendship:

Arthur Lee Adams

Dixie Carter

Wayne Choate

David Kaufman

Ginger Perkins

Lisa Picotte

Larry Randolph

Nancy Reile

Davis Tillman

Vicki & Paul West

"Life ain't in holdin' a good hand.
It's in playin' a pore hand well."

Tilly Mootz, Philosopher

FOREWORD

Throughout our long friendship, I have, along with many others, constantly begged Ronnie Claire to sit down and write her always keen and hilarious observations so everyone could enjoy them, and here at last are the happy results.

The truth is that most writers struggle for years to find and perfect an original and unique voice of their own, but my friend Ronnie Claire has done it, as one of her delightful characters would say, "Right out of the chute."

She is first and foremost a storyteller of the first order with a natural ability to hone in on the quirky and absurd. In fact, it is her enthusiasm for the odd, the eccentric and the strange that puts one in mind of the likes of Flannery O'Connor and Eudora Welty, had they been born West of the Mississippi. But because Ronnie Claire Edwards is a complete original and does not fit easily into any category, the closest way to describe her style is Oklahoma Gothic — if there is such a thing. And if there wasn't, there is now.

Hooray for Ronnie Claire!

Fannie Flagg

THE TRUE STORY
OF THE
KNIFE THROWER'S
ASSISTANT

May 13, 1965

Dear Daughter,

Your mama is concerned about you giving an interview regarding your stint with the knife thrower, fearing it reflects poorly on her parenting. But hell, your great uncle ran a flea circus. You were a step above being dependent on a herd of fleas. You were a solo attraction.

I am as ever, your paw, W.H.E.

and to God, it is true. I really was a knife thrower's assistant. It began thusly: The summer of my fifteenth year, I met "The Great Shoshone Mahaffee, Knife Thrower Extraordinaire." When not hurling them, he also swallowed them and other things, which for the sake of delicacy shall remain nameless.

The Great Shoshone Mahaffee was, as the name implies, half Indian, half Irish, and all drunk. Not a good combination in any profession, but particularly troublesome in a knife thrower. However, the Great Shoshone could charm the skin off a snake, had a keen eye (being half Indian), unswerving aim, a steady hand drunk or sober, and nerves of steel. Not so the knife thrower's assistant, billed as "Fifi, the Female Phenomenon." Fifi was a wan creature with pink cotton candy hair and one of those faces that looked like it hadn't been cooked long enough. She'd been hired because she was just a few shades shy of being an albino, so if she paled in terror the audience couldn't detect it. She also had a cast in one eye that prevented her from seeing the knife coming; but the sound of it had finally gotten to her, causing her to be subject to hysterics during performance. In addition to which she had developed a twitch. But worse yet, the most dangerous of all problems to befall anyone in the knife throwing profession, she had begun to flinch!

5

Part of the requirements of a knife thrower's assistant is having a young nubile body scantily clad in blood red, for obvious reasons, on display in a dangerous situation. It looks good for the act. But due to her increasing bouts of flinching, less and less of Fifi's flesh could be exposed. The cruelest cut of all came when . . . well, let's just say she never again had to worry about a hangnail on her right pinkie finger. So this, coupled with losing her nerve, forced the Great Shoshone to look for new blood.

He hated to turn Fifi loose. He loved her dearly, having found her as a child of fourteen picking peanuts on her father's farm outside Pigg, Arkansas. Her father was loath to see her go because he needed her for the harvest, but the Great Shoshone offered him the money it would cost to hire a hand to do her work if he'd let him have Fifi. Her father jumped at it. He was glad to get rid of another mouth to feed and, besides, her boy cousins were beginning to hang around too much. So The Great Shoshone literally bought her. Now he had to let her go.

Eliza Doolittle, having come up in the world, couldn't go back to Tottenham Court Road any more than Fifi could return to the squalor of Pigg, Arkansas. The Great Shoshone used his influence and got her a job clerking at Liggetts. She cured right up, stopped flinching, married a wealthy podiatrist from Hartshorn, Oklahoma, and was delivered of twins after an eleven-month pregnancy. Rumor has it that they were both born with the last digit missing on their right hands, but that could have been vicious gossip.

6

Here is where I enter the narrative. I had been taking tickets in the tent (anything to be near the world of art) when I sensed the Great Shoshone eyeing me. Not a man to beat around the bush, he approached me straight, and in a very forceful manner told me I had the proper conformation and temperament to train as his assistant! I was thrilled to be noticed by a star of his magnitude, but I demurred, saying that I could never hope to compete with Fifi, the Female Phenomenon. He scoffed at that and swooped me up and fixed me to the apparatus.

The act works like this: the knives are thrown directly at the target. They do not pop up from behind, as the rubes think. It always made me mad when people asked if they did. They must have thought I had no artistic integrity. I was buckled spread-eagle to a wheel by wide leather straps, my head secured in a vise (similar to the electric chair). The climax of the act came when this wheel was given a terrific push and spun as the Great Shoshone commenced hurling knives, swords, sabers, a tomahawk and—the *piece de resistance*—an ax at my rapidly whirling body. Whoever says you cannot hit a moving target is lying. Being a knife thrower's assistant teaches you discipline real fast.

I was determined to be the best in the business. I worked hard and perfected my craft, and, plus my natural ability; I do not believe it is immodest of me to say, as word spread, I became known as the most gifted on the circuit. My star was on the ascendant.

Fame and greatness lay just within my grasp! But alas, it was not meant to be. My career was suddenly and unexpectedly cut short by outside, unseen forces beyond my control. I, unbeknownst to us all, carried within me, like many a creative person, the seeds of my own destruction. In some cases it is the poison drink, Edgar Allan Poe, or the poison of the laudanum poppy, Dante Gabriel Rossetti, but in my case, it was the deadly *Ambrosia traffedia*, common name, ragweed. Nijinsky's fatal flaw was madness, mine was allergies. Oklahoma has the distinction of being the ragweed capital of the world.

We performed in tents. All the heat for hell is warmed up in a tent in Oklahoma in the summer. In order to get air the tent flaps would be raised. Not only was the ragweed in full flower, it was the season for dust storms. Nothing can be more dangerous to a knife thrower's assistant than uncontrollable sneezing. Nature was playing havoc with my sinuses, and they were playing havoc with the act. I had to go. I wept bitter tears. I was covered in shame, dust and pollen. I feared my artistic career was over. How could I ever, after coming so far, so fast, hope to equal my glittering success on that spinning wheel?

Little did I know that summer, as a young girl of fifteen, that a far, far more dangerous fate awaited me, for I was to become an actress!

*　　*　　*

How, you might ask, was a fifteen year old girl from good people allowed to go off with a traveling carnival? It was odd, but not to my folks. But I am getting hind end first. One of my earliest memories was of a carnival banner that screamed, "Lionella!! Alive!!! Why???" over a drawing of a blonde bearded lady. Even at seven years old I knew it was hollering at me. Like Lionella, I too was alive but there was a question of why. Most people could boast, like David Copperfield, "To begin my life with the beginning of my life, I record that I was born." This was not a claim I could make, for I could find no record of my birth. When I inquired as to the whereabouts of a birth certificate, Mama, with a vague wave of her hand, equivocated, "It's around here someplace."

I was aware that although not unwanted, I was an unexpected child. My parents paid to have my older siblings delivered. The doctor had thrown me in for

CLOCKWISE FROM LEFT: OLDER SIBLINGS CAROLINE AND WARREN; MAMA; RONNIE CLAIRE; AND BABY SISTER, HELEN

PAPA, WARREN, OLD COLONEL AND CAROLINE

free on the theory that the carelessness my folks had exhibited in having me would someday repeat itself, and he could charge for the next one. He was right. I have a baby sister. Because I had entered on a free ticket, perhaps the birth certificate was not included.

Papa allowed as how I was born on February eighth. Mama said, "No, Warren, this one was born February ninth. I ought to know. I was there." She always pulled rank on the issue of my birth. As if it weren't bad enough to have a discrepancy in my birth date, they each called me different names! Mama called me Ronnie Claire. Papa called me Sophronia Gertrude, sometimes just Gertie. I answered to all, felt affinity for none. Which one was I? Who was I? I would spend years trying to find out.

First, I sought the meaning of the names. Ronnie is short for Veronica, who gave the cloth to Christ to wipe his brow as he carried the cross. Claire was a Latin name, from St. Clare, the founder of a Franciscan order of nuns, and means bright. Gertrude was a seventh century saint, a mystic. That part I liked. But saints? We were Presbyterian. Sophronia was Greek. Also, Charles Dickens seems to have been fond of it because he used it in several of his novels.

When I asked Mama why Papa called me Sophronia Gertrude, she said, "Just to be perverse." When I asked Papa why Mama called me Ronnie Claire, he said, "Transient apoplexy."

Perhaps I had also identified with Lionella because she seemed so like a family member, a "Human Oddity." My family's eccentricity was God-given, never studied or forced. They were unaware of their peculiarities. Papa cultivated people who were seemingly normal except for singular quirks. It was little wonder he felt at ease with them; he had grown up in a four-story home in Oklahoma City my grandfather had built that housed people who were "turned funny." They could have charged two bits to look at them

Uncle Jim was a licensed medical doctor who preferred to embroider tablecloths. His divorced wife, Ardeeta, lived on the fourth floor and he lived on the third. They had to eat at different times so as not to run into each other.

In the attic lived a Miss Morris, a poetess, who suffered from a nervous disorder that caused her to

UNCLE JIM

claw all the skin off the back of her hands. All her meals were delivered on a tray.

There was the judge who sat on the veranda all day sipping an alcohol based patent medicine, visiting and taking the breeze.

Little Joe Phillips, the child next door, decided at the age of five that he preferred the Edwards to the Phillips and moved in, much to the relief of his family who thought he ate too much. When they moved to Nowata, his mother told my grandmother, "Little Joe is just so happy with you folks, it seems a shame to take him away from you." So Little Joe stayed on through high school.

The hired help consisted of two black cooks and Old Scot, who had been a slave. My grandmother had inherited the care and responsibility of him. She waited on him like a baby. He had no duties except to keep track of her sewing basket. There was also a chauffeur of sorts, Turpentine, who seems to have come with the car when he drove it out from Detroit.

My grandmother had three old-maid half sisters: Modena, Ruth, and Ethel. Modena and Ruth had an ongoing affair with the same man until they all croaked from decrepitude. Ethel early on took a sighting of the lay of the land and her mind went "where the woodbine twineth."

12

There were many incidental characters, coming and going, over the years. Jake Hammond, a horse trader of sorts, liked to touch base, especially when he was flat broke. He'd show up in a chauffeur driven limousine to ask for a loan, "Just to tide me over." For years he worked on a rejuvenating elixir he claimed was a secret recipe he'd gotten off an Indian down in Central America. He wanted to sell my grandfather the franchise for Texas, Oklahoma, and Arkansas. He assured him, "It's a million dollars just around the corner!" Papa said Jake was familiar with the bottom of the deck, that the truth was inadvertent, and he lied just to keep in practice.

Briefly, twin girls stayed with the family. They were called "The Matched Set" or "The Orphans of the Storm" because their parents had been killed in a twister. They had a black cat who ate cigarette butts. Theda Bara had appeared in 1917 in *Under Two Flags* as a heroine named Cigarette, for whom they named the cat. She had only one scrawny grey kitten, probably due to too much nicotine. It was named Smokey.

Of course, none of these disparate personages got along, but the room and eats were free so they all stayed, more or less permanently, with an occasional cast replacement. In order to escape from this bunch and the heat of Oklahoma, the family would travel to the coolness of Montana's Glacier National Park. They were flush with new money, so they often drove huge, eight-passenger touring cars—a Doris or a Stevens-Durray. If when they got to the Cimarron

River it was on the rise, my grandmother, who was used to driving a team of horses, would holler out, "Kick her on in. We'll never get to Montana sitting here."

My aunts and my grandmother covered their faces with whitish calamine lotion to protect themselves from the vicissitudes of riding exposed to the elements in an open touring car for fifteen hundred miles. I'm sure the roads were strewn with the wrecks of oncoming cars, their terrified drivers having caught a glimpse of four white-faced spooks approaching. My Aunt Hortense, who was ten, had to sit on the Books of Knowledge so she could peer over the steering wheel; she did most of the driving along with Papa, who was thirteen, so my grandparents would be free to enjoy and comment on the scenery.

Once while en route they stopped in New Mexico. My grandmother gave an Indian woman a Cain's coffee can and commissioned her to weave a rug with the exact colors that were on the can. On the return trip she stopped to pick up her completed rug. The woman had followed the instructions perfectly. The

14

colors were exact, and beautifully woven in the center were the words, "Cain's Coffee."

For sheer uniqueness, none of the house guests could match the hostess, my grandmother Caroline Hamilton Edwards. Her mother had died when she was three years old, leaving her father to raise her. He brought her to Texas from Mississippi after the War Between

CAROLINE HAMILTON EDWARDS

the States. My grandmother had only faint memories of her mother and would sometimes cry when she spoke of her, not so much over the person of her mother as the pain of growing up without a mother. She adored her father, who was soft-spoken, kind, and courteous, a gentleman.

My grandmother ran off and married Will Edwards because he drove to his buggy a matched set of bay Morgan horses. That had attracted her, coming from a society that knew and loved good horses.

But Will Edwards was nothing like her gentle father. He had a hardness about him and he was driven. The shock of living with a man so different from her father was traumatic for my grandmother; something in her shut down, closed itself off from him. He made three fortunes. She spent them all.

15

PAPA AND HIS SISTERS

Not out of maliciousness but because she had exquisite taste, and her soul cried out for beauty. The buying helped fill the void.

Never having had a mother of her own, my grandmother was ill-equipped to be a mother. She didn't send Papa to school until he was seven so his younger sister would have someone to play with at home. When the family spent the summers in Butte, Montana, they sometimes went in a private railroad car and took a suite of rooms in the best hotel in town. Papa was left to take care of his younger sisters and my grandmother paid no attention to where they went or what they did. And Butte was a rough mining town. It was said that Butte had "three thousand Irishmen: one thousand working the day shift, one thousand working the night shift, and one thousand laying up drunk." These children wandered freely at all hours engaging in their favorite pastimes—climbing on the roofs of the tallest buildings, collecting beer bottles, and hanging around the saloons.

When Papa's two younger sisters were born, he was assigned much of the care of them also. He said, "Mama worked me just like a driven slave." Despite her neglect, Papa loved and respected his mother, but I never saw him kiss her and he was an affectionate man.

Contradictory to my grandmother's sad upbringing she had the ability to make people laugh; all the more so because she was unaware that she was amusing. About a new choir director she commented, "He looks like the kind of young man whose mother had taken him into ladies' restrooms until he was about twelve." In an effort to comfort one of her daughters who was contemplating divorce, she said, "You chose your china, your silver, and your husband all at once and your taste changes."

In the pictures of her as a young woman, she was a strange combination of handsome and delicate with an aristocratic bearing. Her features were not even and, possibly because of this, her face held one's attention. In one portrait she is turned slightly looking directly into the camera almost defiantly. She is wearing a large hat with point d'esprit veiling, a sable coat to the floor, and holding a muff with tails.

By the time I knew her she looked like a cross between Estelle Winwood in the *Madwoman of Chaillot* and Martita Hunt in *Great Expectations*. Her comments were Dickensian, often *sotto voce* behind her hand or veiled by an initialed, embroidered handkerchief which lent to even the most mundane utterances great drama and suspense. She spoke of subjects shrouded in mystery. "If the girl had been interfered with, from whom does the proposed offspring emanate?"

Her gestures were extravagant, fluid, as innately melodramatic as a diva's, yet in no way did they seem artificial but natural to her. She would clutch her breast and throw her head back, hand to brow; or draw away, holding her arms rigidly in front of her, palms out as if she were recoiling from some horror.

She enjoyed telling about (and I loved hearing about) Sister Aimee Semple McPherson. She first saw her at The Four Square Gospel Tabernacle, in Los Angeles' Echo Park. She presented pageants and recitals. She came down a winding stairway carrying four dozen red roses, dressed in flowing white robes. My grandmother said, "Solomon in all his glory was not arrayed so fine. Everything was on display except a choir of naked angels." Sister Aimee's sermons spoke of being on the toboggan slide to hell, riding the hoot owl trail, folks going through more sin than a good preacher could pray them out of. She exhorted her flock to turn their backs on sin and let the Holy Ghost conviction grip them. She said she hated sin worse than the devil hates holy water and claimed she couldn't wait to go up in the Rapture.

When my grandmother went to Hawaii on the Luriline, Sister Aimee was on board. She had cast aside her priestly raiments. My grandmother said she had on a dress that "didn't have enough fabric in it to pad a crutch, but she must have figured it was all right because she was out past the twelve-mile limit."

My grandmother claimed she noticed the Lord manifested Himself to people and they got salvation when they were facing eight to ten for income tax evasion.

She was constantly pointing out to me what people wore, what their clothing revealed about them. Her weird and wonderful observations came from an ability to fasten onto the tiniest detail, an artist who sees the shadow the rest of us can't see. She believed in phrenology—a person's physical characteristics indicated their character. These judgments were made instantaneously and with complete authority. She would shamelessly stare with the concentration of an animal stalking prey, then take a deep breath, having grasped it and, turn away and make her pronunciamento.

She feared the loss of her senses and told me, "When I was a girl, I could remember everything whether it happened or not. My hearing was so acute I could hear a doodlebug land on a bale of cotton. Now I miss my ears, my eyes, but most of all I miss my mind."

The day before she had her teeth pulled she confided to me, "The jury has brought in its verdict. The judge has gaveled down my sentence. I know now how the condemned feel facing the hangman's noose. The only difference being I am unable to eat my last meal!"

After seeing Jackie Kennedy on television, she

said, "What a fascinating, phenomenal, physical flaw she has. One heretofore I have never witnessed. She has an eye over each ear, thereby making it impossible for them both to focus on the same object at once. I am at a loss as to what this portends."

Even now, when I walk on a soft carpet I remember her describing her similar experience as "like walking on house cats." I can never wear brown because of her admonition. "Brown can be smart, but never pretty." Sometimes when I am attracted to some new just-out article, her voice reminds me, "The fad is what the well-dressed woman is not wearing this year."

She encouraged me early on to absorb and detect the singular in people, never to point or laugh, never flinch from sights that might make others cross the road, never turn my back or a blind eye on the strange, because that type of squeamishness would limit my world.

She was the embodiment of the Del Sarte Method, having a gesture for every emotion. With such a grandmother, is it any wonder I became an actress?

*   *   *

All of these characters and events were on the easily recalled surface of my mind. It was not until I got the ocular proof of so many more people that I went deep into memory. This did not happen until Mama and Papa were both gone and my siblings shipped me all the things they didn't want but couldn't bear to throw out.

*   *   *

What is to be done with the belongings of three generations? China teacups with broken handles, mismatched chipped goblets, dozens of handkerchiefs and yellowed pillow cases edged with my great grandmother's tatting, Papa's white butcher linen suits, and fringed gauntlet gloves he'd given Mama made from the hide of a deer he'd shot in Montana the first year they were married. There were boxes of white baby clothes with tiny handmade tucks, trimmed in Irish lace and disintegrating love knots of silk ribbon, and doll clothes made as beautifully as the baby clothes. Many little girls' dresses with ruched yokes and panties to match. Even a box of baby didies. My parents' marriage license, baby shoes, Eastern Star pins, and framed pictures of my great uncles in their Masonic aprons. In the bottom of the box, wrapped in a Texas Star patterned quilt, was a blue velvet-covered family album with a brass clasp. Out of the gold-edged cutouts stare grim ancestors. Tucked in the back of the album was a stack of Confederate money tied with a strip of homespun cloth. Loose tintypes fell out, one a picture of a dead infant in a coffin. On the back is written, "Little Lorena. Two years, three months. She is with the angels now."

All this had been thrown in higgley piggledy with

no order or care. I thought I might paw through to my birth certificate.

The shipping company had labeled the boxes in "LOTS." A family's history, my people's lives, and my life were contained in those boxes. What secrets did they hold, of matters spoken of *sotto voce*, and were hushed when a child entered the room? I felt responsible for those past generation's belongings, having been given the things they had treasured. What would I discover about them? Would I find my birth certificate or something more important . . . myself?

LOT 104

THE APPRENTICE ADVENTURESS

"R.C.E. Melodrama" was scrawled across the lid of the box. Inside I found long, skinny tear sheets of newsprint rolled up with a rotten rubber band that snapped when I pulled it. The paper retained its curl. I smoothed the roll flat to find programs in faded colors: pink, green, orange, blue, in many different type styles. On each sheet a different melodrama was listed. "The Imperial Players proudly present 'THE FLYING SCUD OR A FOUR LEGGED FORTUNE,' 'HAZEL KIRK OR ADRIFT FROM HER FATHER'S LOVE,' 'SWEENEY TODD, DEMON BARBER OF FLEET STREET' ...Matinees and Evening Performances Tuesday Thru Sunday, 2:00 & 8:00 ... Followed by Olio Acts in the Sluice Saloon."

I was seventeen when I shook the dust from my heels and headed for higher ground. My destination was a mining camp, a fifty-four hour bus ride from Oklahoma City. Because I had never been that far away from home before, I took everything I owned: picture hats, organdy dresses, white gloves all packed in cardboard boxes. It turned out I had no use for these ensembles, since the actors lived in tents in Fool's Gold Gulch. We called ourselves "The Pyrites."

We performed for the tourists, twelve shows a week! I survived it because I was a kid. It taught me my business. No one can be on stage twice a day for thirteen weeks and not learn a little something. An actress learns the same way as a dog and a dimwit, by going over and over and over it. Rich kids were sent to summer camp; I spent my summer in a mining camp.

The woman who owned the opera house and the adjoining Sluice Saloon was referred to as "The Empresariess of the Mining Camp." She stood in the lobby and greeted the patrons. It was her domain, and she ruled it with the glamour and style of Joan Crawford and the air and command of a circus ringmaster. She was tall, with a lovely figure, had pale skin, and wore her auburn hair in an upsweep. She affected a flowing Isadora Duncan scarf and wore a ring with a big yellow, many-faceted stone she called "my brandy diamond." She smoked long, thin, black cigarillos. Despite her appearance, there was nothing remotely romantic about her personae. She was a savvy businesswoman who knew when a bartender started taking from the till and how much, and she could fire an actor mid-season. I was terrified of her. Her office had a globe chandelier, a mahogany secretary, oil paintings, velvet fringed portieres, and an Oriental carpet. Beautiful as it was, none of the actors wanted to be called in on that carpet.

Our dressing rooms below stage were papered with worthless gold mine stock certificates. What had at one time represented millions in gold covered the walls and ceiling with beautiful, ornate lettering and etchings depicting mine sites. I loved the names: the Molly Kathleen, the Jim Dandy, the Copa de Oro, the Matchless, the Phoenix, the Lucky Pit, the Royal Flush.

In addition to the melodramas, we declaimed narrative poems. "The Face On The Barroom Floor, "The Cremation of Sam McGee," and "Casey At The Bat." We also sang "She's More To Be Pitied Than Censored," "My Mother Was A Lady," "After The Ball," and "My Evenin' Star." I sat on an upright piano wearing a black satin dress and a molting feather boa, both reeking of stale toilet water worn by actresses in seasons past. I am what is known as a "Methodist soprano," so I sang in a thin, tiny voice with wavering pitch:

> You've made me what I am today,
> I hope you're satisfied.
> You've dragged and dragged me down until
> The soul within me died.
> You've shattered each and every dream,
> You've fooled me from the start,
> And though you're not true
> May God bless you.
> That's the curse of an aching heart.

Between acts, we presented tableaux. I sat upstage center, awash in a bastard amber light, draped in a Grecian ensemble, and clutching a bundle. An actor garbed in an artist's smock, holding a paint brush, recited:

> I hailed me a woman from the street,

Shameless, but oh, so fair!
I bade her sit in the model's seat
And I painted her sitting there.

I hid all trace of her heart unclean;
I painted a babe at her breast.
I painted her as she might have been:
If the Worst had been the Best.

She laughed at my picture and went away,
Then came with a knowing nod,
A connoisseur, and I heard him say;
"'Tis Mary, the Mother of God."

So I painted a halo round her hair.
And I sold her and took my fee,
And she hangs in the church of Saint Hilaire,
Where you and all may see.

Nancy Doyle played the engenue roles. In the olio act she sang "Oceana Roll," dressed in a blue satin sailor suit. Her father was a psychiatrist at the Arizona asylum that housed Winnie Ruth Judd, the famous trunk murderess. Winnie Ruth kept getting out and wandering around loose, sometimes for years. Dr. Doyle let Nancy eat brownies Winnie Ruth made for his family because he said there was no reason to be scared of her.

The costumer was an admirable lady with the wondrous name of Wenonah Poindexter. Her father had performed chalk talks on the Chautauqua circuit. Chalk talks were just what the name implies. A performer, often billed as "The Professor," would stand

R.C.E. BEING OUTFITTED BY WENONAH POINDEXTER

on a stage with a blackboard or a large tablet on an easel and a box of chalk. As he recited :

"The stag at eve had drunk it's fill
Where danced the moon on Monan's Rill"

before the audience's very eyes he drew the majestic stag, antlers and all. Or:

"'Neath the spreading chestnut tree,
The village smithy stands."

And behold! There he stood, anvil and tongs. Or:

"Listen, my children, and you shall hear,
Of the midnight ride of Paul Revere,"

And there raced the hero of the Revolution, astride his galloping steed, lantern held aloft.

I asked Wenonah how she got her name. She told me one of her father's selections was "Hiawatha."

"In the moonlight and the starlight,
Fair Nokomis bore a daughter.
And she called her Wenonah."

It seems Longfellow's Wenonah "got in trouble with the wind" and bore Hiawatha.

      ✻   **✻**   **✻**

Although there were fewer than two hundred residents, the mining camp had an abundance of "odd lot" people. One old fellow wore a cap with a carbide lamp, and in exchange for sweeping the lobby he'd persuaded the Empresariess to let him participate when "The Shooting of Dan McGrew" was performed. Just at the moment when the actor declaimed, "Then I ducked my head and the lights went out and two guns blazed in the dark," the old man would leap to his feet in the back of the house and fire off a derringer. It infuriated the actor, because his lines were never heard.

Shooting off guns in public places was common practice in the mining camps at the turn of the century. Troops of strolling players would come through and sometimes, being short of actors for all the roles, they would hire townspeople for some of the parts. One night in the course of the drama, a scene required an actor to stab a woman on stage, and one of the old miners leapt up and fired off a bullet, barely missing the leading man, hollering, "You son of a bitch! You've killed the only whore in Jackass Flats!"

The summer I was there one of the most pitiful residents was a tiny child we called Little Bit, who stationed herself outside the swinging doors of the Sluice Saloon. In her grimy little hands she clutched a cigar box marked "rocs 5¢." It was filled with bits of pyrite, turquoise, minuscule garnets, and quartz chips. Rumor had it that she was incestuously begot, and she seemed to be the sole support of a father crippled in the mines. He pushed himself around town on a homemade cart with his gloved hands. I would bring Little Bit candy and try to engage her in conversation. She never responded. I assumed she was mute. Late one night I heard what sounded like a kitten, and there in the alley behind the saloon crouched Little Bit. She was feeding broken pieces of candy to a half-starved kitten. It was her mewing I'd heard. When I walked past her, she never looked up.

Mining camps are steeped in tales of men gone mad in the bowels of the earth, riches beyond avarice, suicides when a gold vein played out, "soiled doves" with hearts of gold, and homeless waifs. Little Bit had many predecessors. One tale was of a poor, semi-orphaned child on the edge of womanhood who lived in a miner's shack with her father. He drank like a suction hose, and was said to beat her only when he was drunk. Giving the devil his due, to his credit he took pride in his paternal priority. He did-n't allow anyone else to beat up on her. The child swept saloons, wiped the bars, polished the brass rails, and emptied the slops from upstairs. She wore a gunny sack dress and a coat cut from a wagon sheet; but like the figure in the poem, "She walked in beauty like the night," for on her feet she wore a pair of paisley Turkish slippers, tipped at the curled toes by tiny tinkling brass bells, a gift from one of the girls upstairs — a pretty, pale consumptive creature who called herself Cereus after the fragrant flower of the cactus which bloomed only at night. Often Cereus would escape to the Chinatown section where she exchanged herself for the hazy trance of the opium pipe. It was said this gift of the slippers, a gift of such kindness and beauty, so touched the child that she became enamored of the pale whore and began to fantasize of a life over the saloon. One day Cereus leaned over the railing and called down to the child, motioning for her to come up. The child, flushed with pleasure, wiped her raw, chapped hands on her rough dress and followed Cereus with anticipation down the long, dark hall to her room. Cereus wordlessly motioned for her to sit on the iron bed. Perhaps the child prayed, held her breath, hoping for some other glittering gift to match her wondrous, tinkling slippers. Instead, Cereus turned to her and dropped her wrapper to her waist exposing her beautiful blue-veined, pale as skim milk bosom, throat, arms, and shoulders, where the bruises and teeth marks of a dozen different men flowered. Pointing toward the door, she said to the child, "Go."

Although these girls' lives were pitiable and sordid, not all ended sadly. A case in point was the tale of Big Faye, who dressed out at about 250. She worked the fandango halls and one night during one of the frequent brawls, Big Faye was shot, but the bullet couldn't get through to the vitals. There was a subsequent trial where the judge looked down and asked, "Were you wounded in the fracas?" Big Faye looked up and in a small, pious voice, responded, "No, Your Honor. It was somewhere between the knee and the fracas."

When Big Faye had recovered, she returned to the fandango hall where, while dancing the polka, a tiny, red-headed Irishman no bigger than a leprechaun fell madly in love with her. He owned a big hotel in the middle of Last Chance Gulch in Missoula, Montana. The nuptial date was set and Big Faye wanted to lose some poundage for the wedding. After she'd shed about fifty pounds, the little Irishman sensed something was amiss. When Big Faye confessed her weight loss, he pitched a fit, stamping his tiny feet and tearing at his red hair. So Big Faye dutifully put the pounds back on.

After about two wedded years, the bliss began to wear thin. Big Faye was bored with just one man. She missed the girls and the life, so to keep her company the little Irishman sent for some of her co-workers from the fandango hall to work his hotel. Rumor had it she lived fat and rich in a long, happy marriage with her little Irishman.

* * *

We worked so hard and such long hours that the Impresariess must have assumed we had no energy left to go astray, or perhaps she was too exhausted to care. We certainly had no supervision. I took advantage of this and was lucky. She never caught me. Some of my adventures were terrifying in their boldness. They were foolhardy and dangerous, yet I was never frightened. At seventeen, I wasn't scared of the devil himself.

The floor over the saloon was off limits. We had been warned that it was rotted and would not bear weight. The door at the top of the stairs was nailed shut and all the windows were boarded. What could have been more tempting? Rickety wooden steps led from the alley to this top story. The padlock on the door was rusted. All was closed and quiet on Mondays, our day off, so I felt safe when I climbed the steps. When I pushed on the door it opened inward with a scraping sound, causing me to fall forward into total darkness. I had brought a flashlight and felt like Nancy Drew.

The boards groaned under my weight, as I picked my way over the floor littered with broken whiskey bottles and rat droppings. A man's cracked boot lay amidst the rubble. There were doors on both sides of the long, narrow hallway, some standing open. From cracks in the boarded windows escaped spears of light with floating dust motes. I began to sneeze, which was a blessing because my nose stopped up and I could no longer smell the stale rancid, sweet-sour stench.

In one room was an iron bed with a stained cotton mattress, and on it was a blue bottle labeled "Dr. Weir's Lotion for Crab Lice." In a room three doors down, cerise tarlatan curtains hung in shreds, their black balled fringe tangled on the floor.

My flashlight beam danced over the doors picking out the names Birdie, Lola, Mildred, and Gussie. I wandered down the hall and pushed open the door to the last room. It was empty, but I noticed something in the corner. It was a paper fan, and it broke away from the ribs when I opened it. Drawn on it was an Oriental couple engaged in an erotic act. As I left the room, the flashlight picked up the name above the door—Cereus. So the story was true.

I retraced my steps and went out into the bright day, closing the door on these sad little ghosts. I told the Empresariess about the broken lock. The next week, I noticed it had been replaced.

Although I'd closed the door on the ghosts, I couldn't close my mind on them. Throughout the summer I wondered about their names. Was Birdie so named because she was tiny, with fluttery movements? Was she nervous? Did she indulge in laudanum from time to time to calm herself? Was Lola a Mexican? Working over a saloon must have seemed like heaven after walking the Avenida de Juarez. Mildred—such a solid, farm girl name. Did Gussie rig herself out in cheap finery to get all "gussied up"?

Going through Lot 104, I found the broken fan with the drawing of the Oriental couple wrapped in a Sluice Saloon napkin.

*　　*　　*

In a cigar box were tubes of Stein's Grease Paint still oozing grease, snarled hairpieces of assorted shades, dried up lipsticks, and false eyelashes stuck together. Deeper in the box were tights with one purple leg and one red leg with nothing left but the runs, crumbling rubber falsies, a broken egret feather, mismatched dangling earrings, and a tambourine with ribbons. Tossed among all this mess were letters from Papa addressed to me at many different theaters.

I excavated through the corselets, the orange high-top shoes, the Spanish shawl with the tangled fringe, the shredded tarlatan petticoats, a crushed picture hat—all the remnants of those long-ago theatrical beginnings when I thought, like every young actress, that the theater was out there waiting for me and was mine for the taking.

I felt something slick. It was a glossy 8 x 10 photo, cracked down the center. Given the subject, the crack was appropriate.

On our day off, the cast would often travel to the nearest big town if we could persuade the Empresariess to let us use the company truck. Coming back late one night, we had a flat tire. We sat freezing for a couple of hours in the flatbed. Finally we saw headlights of an old limousine. It stopped, and as we approached it, the window was rolled down a crack. We explained that we were actors from the melodrama and a voice such as I had never heard before — high, hoarse, barely above a whisper — instructed us to get in the back seat. A Roman shade closed us off from the driver. We rode in silence and were let out at the edge of town.

I later learned that the driver lived in a ghost town seven miles away. I was haunted by the experience, so a few weeks later on my night off, I took the narrow gauge railroad that stopped there.

I wandered around and saw not a soul; the town was deserted. There was a large, ramshackle house on a slight rise overlooking the town. As I came on it at dusk, it was in shadow. Two sets of antlers rose from the ground near the front walkway. Drawing closer, I saw that they were toppled iron statues of deer that must have flanked the gate.

The grounds were covered in a species of plant called datura. The formal gardens were overgrown with poisonous jimson weed, and the Gothic columns were strangled with morning glory vines, their trumpet-shaped flowers closing as night came on. At the end of the veranda was a deadly nightshade, sometimes called bella donna, used by Victorian ladies as eyedrops to dilate the pupils of their eyes and make them shine.

The railings and steps had crumbled. Turning to go, I was startled to see a faint light. I picked my way precariously across the rotting porch and as I reached for the knocker the door flew open. I stood face to face with an apparition, and I knew when he said, "Yes?" in a whispery voice, that I had found who I came for. I said I had come to thank him for picking up the actors. There was a long silence and he asked me to come in.

With the door shut, it was dark except for the lone candle he carried. He proceeded around the room, lighting iron torcheres. Slowly, as each area was illuminated, the room and its contents were revealed. It resembled a banquet hall. On either side of the door were floor to ceiling windows draped in red velour which had faded in streaks. In the gloom I saw a Turkish corner, piled with overlapping rugs, a water pipe, swags of tassels and a cloisonne vase of peacock feathers. The main part of the room had iron garden furniture in the shape of curling vines and twisting twigs. A tarnished brass bed with a fur coverlet was piled high with pillows of cheap satin and fringe.

The torcheres gave enough light that I could now get a look at my host. He wore a turban of indeterminate color, shot through with gold, and a purple velvet monk's robe with full loose sleeves lined in rotted silk. The robe flowed from a yoke embroidered with odd symbols seen on the costumes of fraternal orders. On his feet were beaded Chinese scuffs.

His fingers were long and slender with manicured nails. His face was genderless, old but devoid of wrinkles, like a blank sheet. It was the pale, waxy color of some Orientals. His eyes were large, green, luminous—appearing to be all pupil encircled with smudged kohl. The expression was puzzled, childlike, and sad. He possessed a grace, a shy dignity, and was completely androgynous.

He indicated for me to sit on a garden bench. I heard something stir in the corner and recognized the dwarf from the mining camp. He was blind and was called "the Mole" because he ran the tourist concession in the Mattrix Mine. My host referred to him as "my assistant."

He gave instructions and the Mole left the room, returning in a few minutes with a set of Nippon cups and a teapot in the shape of a dragon, its scaly tail the handle and its mouth the spout. My host poured tea as beautifully as any geisha. His incredible eyes never left my face, and he seldom blinked, and even then slowly, like a reptile.

When I inquired what was in the rest of the building, he rose, and the dwarf rose at the same time, and preceded us holding a candelabra; we trailed after him, a phantasmagorical procession. The Mole opened a set of pocket doors revealing an immense room, ringed around the top by a banistered balcony. Hanging from it were what appeared to be spangled costumes, glittering faintly in the dim light, and large canvas banners so weathered that the orange lettering could not be deciphered.

We progressed deeper into the room, the dwarf leading us. At the far end he lit an altar of candles which threw light on a faded painted banner at least ten feet high suspended by ropes laced through leather grommets and stretched taut to the banisters. On the banner was a garish painting of a person, one side of its body dressed in a tuxedo, the other side in an evening gown. Across the top was lettered "MYSTERY! MICHAEL OR MICHELLE?" and across the bottom, "GOD'S MIRACLE OR MISTAKE?"

Nothing was said as we walked back into the entry room. I said I should go because I didn't want to miss the train. He insisted that he drive me back. This time the Roman shade was raised.

We drove in silence. He let me out at the edge of the mining camp. As I turned to go, he grabbed my hand. Startled, I looked into his strange eyes. From inside his sleeve, he pulled something out and pushed it into my hand.

When I got back to my room, I saw that it was a faded, glossy photo of my host. Across the bottom, in spidery script, was written, "To my fellow artist. Best wishes, Michael Michelle, God's Miracle."

These two outcasts, the sideshow anomaly and the dwarf, had found comfort and solace in one another's companionship. I felt privileged to have been allowed into their sanctum sanctorum. I never revealed my visit to anyone.

I realize now that some of the happiest days of my life were spent in that mining camp. What a gift the Empresariess had given me, with and without her knowing it. My life off stage that summer reflected my life on stage, but no melodrama could have equaled my true adventures.

Before I closed the box, I took out a program that read, "NO MOTHER TO GUIDE HER. See the heroine struggle with HARROWING, PERILOUS, DEATH DEFYING ESCAPADES where she is snatched from the JAWS OF DEATH. Those who hear the tale told will THRILL with HORROR and MELT with PITY at what takes place! It will STUN the beholder, APPALL the imagination, and CHILL THE BLOOD!!! Featuring Miss Ronnie Claire Edwards as an ADVENTURESS!!" How true.

July 10, 1977

My Darling Gerty:

We received a letter from you saying that you passed a written test for learning to drive a car. My first suggestion to you is that you buy a transport truck for the simple reason that you have your trash scattered from Dallas to Oklahoma City to New York City to Switzerland to Los Angeles and anywhere else you may have stopped in the last five years.

Also, I caution you very strongly that, at your advanced age, I doubt you will ever learn to drive any kind of vehicle, horse-drawn or otherwise, for the simple reason that neither your mother or your grandmothers had the mental qualifications to learn how to herd an automobile. Such weak-mindedness is generally an inherited characteristic.

If you ever try to drive a car or a truck on the highway, please remember, if you can, that when you meet an oncoming vehicle, you are not supposed to meet it head-on, but pull to the right so you will not hit it. Also, do not do like your mother does when she starts to pass a transport truck. She tries to pass it in the same lane it is in, which is not practical.

I am, as ever, your Paw.
W.H.E.

LOT 109

Curs, Critters and Varmints

n the top were shoe boxes overflowing with jumbled snapshots, as if the subjects' were so frenzied and disordered that they couldn't be contained and seemed to cry out, "Choose me!" "Choose me!" There were scrapbooks of black construction paper, the corners of the pictures stuck in little triangles, initials and dates written in white ink under them. Dozens of pictures of generations of children in Halloween and dance recital costumes, blowing out candles on birthday cakes, opening Christmas presents, couples on trips to Old Mexico, Carlsbad Caverns, the Grand Canyon, and men with their hats off in front of the Alamo. There were studio portraits of my aunts in glamorous poses. A tinted picture of Aunt Hortense, who was Queen-of-the-Fairies beautiful, with big grey eyes, a mass of honey-colored hair, and a willowy figure. She was called "Heavenly Hortense." Papa's youngest sister, Lillian, in her portrait is wearing a black velvet, silk-backed, cut-on-the-bias dress with ermine cuffs ten inches deep. On the back of the portrait is written, "The photographer told me I looked like Nazimova, and I believed him!" Another sister, because of her intelligence, was referred to as "the Oracle of Delphi." These names were not given to the girls as a joke, but rather because it was felt they so richly deserved them.

In many of the loose snapshots, people were pictured with dogs, cats, rabbits, guinea pigs, pigeons, horny toads, a possum with babies hanging on her tail, a raccoon, horses, ponies, and an armadillo. Several of the snapshots were of young children piled into a go-cart harnessed to a goat. Another showed a baby wearing a huge lace bonnet in a wagon surrounded by pups. Written in barely discernible pencil, on the backs of the pictures were the initials, C.P. with Trixie, C.P. with Sponge Budge, W.W. with Colonel, H.M. with Spic n'Span, R.C. with Thomasina, W.W. on Rex, R.C. on Old Paint, C.P. with Dixie, H.M. with Little Earle, W.H. with Dixie Jr." It was assumed that future generations would know who the initials stood for, but the animals had to be named so they would be remembered too. Papa once said, for the money he'd spent on vet bills he could have put the dogs up in a private room at Baptist Hospital with a round-the-clock nurse.

There was a picture of a tiny woman, Miz Arnette, with a monkey perched on her shoulder, its tail wrapped around her neck.

She and the monkey resembled one another. She lived in the upstairs duplex next to my grandparents. I remember everything about her. She had seemed ageless, and could have been anywhere from 40 to 70. It was appropriate that she would have a monkey, as she affected the exotic in all ways.

Miz Arnette always wore a Japanese kimono. She had dozens. Because she never dressed to go out, I thought she was an invalid. Sometimes she threw a

48

piano shawl or a Spanish mantilla over her shoulders. She had enormous black eyes and lashes thickly beaded with Maybelline mascara, the cake kind you have to spit on. She anointed herself heavily with Shalimar perfume. Her hair was gorgeous and heavy, jet black with just the beginning streaks of grey. It was parted in the middle and marcelled close to her scalp and hung loose down her back past her waist. Sometimes she wore it in a plait in which she fastened bits of iridescent peacock feathers, a single jeweled earring, or paper serpentine streamers, the kind people throw on New Year's Eve. On the top of her head were two crossed pencils, like chopsticks.

Miz Arnette's hands were claws, horribly crippled with arthritis. Her fingers were stained with ink and her long nails were painted with Helena Rubenstein's Black Orchid polish. She wore many rings on every finger, gypsy earrings, and a bracelet with the head of a raised cobra. She was always bare-footed. Her tiny, arthritic feet resembled the bound feet of Chinese concubines, and her toenails clicked on the floor when she walked.

About 10:30 every morning (she was a late riser, having been up half the night in scholarly pursuits), without knocking she would enter my grandmother's kitchen for the first of her numerous cups of strong, black coffee. She would light up her first Turkish cigarette of the day, which she smoked from an orange and black lacquer Art Deco holder.

Accompanying Miz Arnette was Little Lucifer, a tiny monkey of the hurdy gurdy species. His chain had the same decorations as her braid. He was allowed the run of the house and had a bad habit of doing his business out of sight, which Miz Arnette feigned ignorance of. This did not endear him to the help when they cleaned behind the davenport. When my aunt was married at home, Little Lucifer was dressed for the occasion in a rhinestone necklace as a collar and was chained outside to the clothesline. Accustomed to having the run of the place, and considering himself an indoor monkey, he protested loudly all through the ceremony.

Miz Arnette often carried in one hand a large sheaf of poorly organized papers covered in a huge, illegible scrawl, and in the other hand, the Bible. For Miz Arnette had a mission, a calling, a *raison d'être*. She was rewriting the Old Testament. The New Testament she dismissed as lacking antiquity, plus she believed in a vengeful God. This was not a project one could do haphazardly or quickly. It was a life's work. She was only a third of the way through Deuteronomy, and she had been at it 20 years. I often wondered why my Biblical quotes were reacted to curiously until I realized they were not from the King James Version, but from the Arnette Version.

In my family, Miz Arnette was not considered or treated as an oddity. As a child I thought her as beautiful and alluring as a princess out of the Arabian Nights. I loved her haughtiness, her imperiousness, her high-strung artistic temperament, and, of course, Little Lucifer.

Then, one morning she didn't enter my grandmother's kitchen. Poof! She was gone. All my queries were brushed aside with vague explanations.

Twenty-five years later, I learned the cause of her disappearance and her whereabouts. It seems she had become "unmanageable."

To whom? She had been confined to the insane asylum at Norman. Her version of the Old Testament had been used against her and discarded as the ravings of a maniac. Her glorious hair was shorn. Gone were her kimonos, the Art Deco cigarette holder, the snake bracelet, and Little Lucifer. Divested of her wondrous trappings and her life's work, she sank into melancholia and was dead within a year.

Oh, Miz Arnette, I treasure your memory. "You are such stuff as dreams are made on."

*   *   *

There was a snapshot of Papa holding the head of a dead snake and Slim Rorem holding the tail. On the back was written, "Okeene, Oklahoma Rattlesnake Roundup. 1942. 6 feet, 4 inches, 5 rattles."

Papa had at one time boarded horses with Slim, who had a falling- down barn and some good grazing land. Slim, as the name implies, had just that—a cowboy build and a rough charm.

Mrs. Rorem had a sweet, pretty face, wore black oxfords, and her red hair in a bun. She had tiny hands and feet attached to a 200-pound body. She was well-educated and taught school. Slim hadn't finished sixth grade. This bothered Mama. "Why would she marry him?"

Papa replied, "God of Israel, Pauline. It's obvious."

The Rorems lived in a red rock house on a piece of low land surrounded by trees. They never seemed to have any visible means of support other than Mrs. Rorem's salary from substitute teaching. I was warned never to go into the woods because it was full of ticks. I suspect the real reason was because Slim was doing a little bootlegging and he kept his whiskey there.

The Rorems spent their vacation the same way every year. They'd get in their pickup, pulling a horse trailer which held their tent and gear. It couldn't be put in the bed of the pickup because that was full of rocks and trash Slim had accumulated over the years. They would go to the Rattlesnake Roundup in Okeene, Oklahoma, and camp out.

Slim told people, "I'm not a snake handler. I'm a snake hunter." And he'd roar with laughter. This was his idea of a joke. Slim was driven by the ambition to catch the most snakes so he could be named Top Rattler Wrangler.

When Papa was county attorney, he made Slim a deputy because he felt sorry for Mrs. Rorem having to do all the work. Slim never stopped hounding Papa to give him the money to set him up in business. His plan was to go to New Mexico and open a rock shop and snake farm tourist attraction. He'd get Mrs. Rorem to work out the figures on a Big Chief tablet to show how it could be a success. Finally he wore Papa down, so Papa gave him a little money just to shut him up. Mama was furious.

Years later, when I planned to drive across the country, Papa told me to stop in New Mexico, and "Check on my investment."

Outside of Tucumcari, I began to see weathered signs. ROREM'S REPTILE RANCH, RATTLERS!, GILA MONSTERS!, " 'WHAT IS IT?'! I finally found the place just as it was getting dark. Inside it was still hot as hell, and there sat Slim in a wheelchair, coughing and smoking a Phillip Morris. He was watching *The Laurence Welk Show* on a twelve-inch TV. The black and white screen flickered and rolled.He remembered me after I told him who I was. He said he was "All stove up with the arthritis." I inquired after Mrs. Rorem. He said she was out back, feeding mice to the snakes. So things hadn't changed. She was still doing all the work.

I asked how business was and he said, "It's all shot to hell since the interstate passed us, but me and Mrs. Rorem are thinking of selling out and moving to Florida to open up a bait shop and Dairy Queen. You don't suppose your father would want to be cut in on it, do you?" I said I didn't think so.

*   *   *

Wrapped with a piece of twine were several pictures of the same subject in different poses. Dog jumping through a hoop, dog standing on its hind legs, dog playing dead. They were of my Aunt Erma,

AUNT ERMA

myself, and Renata putting Zinkie through her repertoire of tricks.

My Aunt Erma was almost defenseless; she had been crippled since childhood from what the doctors later suspected was infantile paralysis and she walked with a severe limp. Because her husband worked on the night crew at the railroad yard, she needed someone to stay with her. The person they chose was ill suited for the job, a young woman barely out of her teens, a little bit of a thing who couldn't have fought off a gnat. Her name was Renata and she came from a wide place in the road in southern Oklahoma called Little Dixie because it was filled with Baptists who voted the straight Democratic ticket.

Renata had raging red hair, and lots of it. It looked like it would itch you if you touched it. It was so kinky, so wiry, that the ends must have never seen the light of day, since as soon as they sprouted, they whirled and twirled and squished right back to her scalp, doubling up on themselves. It was a downright affliction. When she cleaned her room, in the hope of containing it she would tie a bandana around her head so tight it made her eyes bug out. All to no avail, because before you could say "Jack Robinson," here it came. At first a bit of fuzz, then tiny hairs joined by a strand, until it all escaped and circled her face like a poke bonnet. She couldn't have gotten her head in a bushel basket. Her skin was given to breaking out in a heat rash, its color almost matching her hair. Summers in Oklahoma could be a problem. And she had an overbite, in other words she was buck-toothed. Papa said, "That young woman has got a mouth like a bottle opener."

Renata had a huge guffaw of a laugh. Hearing her "Har, har, har" took people by surprise, coming from such a tiny thing. But despite her downright weird appearance, Renata had charm, appeal, and was fun to be around. And strange as it seems, she was attractive.

These two innocents, my crippled aunt and this odd little country girl, somehow felt safe together. On Saturday afternoons we'd sit around the Philco radio and listen to the Metropolitan Opera broadcasts. Aunt Erma liked Lily Pons best, but Renata and I preferred Gladys Swarthout in *Carmen*.

Aunt Erma would phone Veazey Drugstore and order two cherry phosphates with lots of chipped ice, one for me and one for herself, and a R.C. Cola for Renata. These were the days when a delivery boy would peddle his bike miles in the broiling heat to deliver a 30-cent order for a nickel tip. Renata always threw a couple of aspirin and some peanuts in the R.C. Cola bottle, shook it up, and then quick, put it in her mouth to catch the fizz. She was the first person I ever knew to do this. She said it gave her a kind of a pickup.

Then we'd eat rat cheese on soda crackers and Fig Newtons. These refreshments were timed to be eaten during the opera intermissions when Milton Cross came on, to make us feel like we were actually there at the opera.

During the long afternoon performances, Aunt Erma taught me to embroider and Renata taught me to crochet. Aunt Erma said a lady had to always have "lap work." When not instructing me, they instructed Zinkie how to jump through the embroidery hoop. He was half Mexican Hairless and half Toy Wire Haired Terrier. He was named for the Diva, Zinka Milinof. Zinkie looked like he started out one way and then nature changed its mind. True to his descriptive breed types, he had wire-haired ears, a beard, and a body patchily covered in weird looking hair, almost as weird as Renata's. He had raw looking hairless legs and a long tail, naked as a rat's. Zinkie and Renata were equivalent in size for their individual species.

It was Renata who took me to the state fair every year. First stop, the hog barn, where we marveled at the huge sows, with suckling piglets so pink and adorable. It was not just the cuteness of the shoats that drew us, but the sight of their mother, her enormity which bordered on freakishness, and we loved freaks! I once made the mistake of reaching in to pick up a piglet. The sow let out an ear-splitting squeal, launched her huge bulk up on to her tiny feet with amazing agility, and charged. We tore out of the barn, terrified.

After fortifying ourselves with enough cotton candy, lemonade, and Crackerjacks to assure that we'd be sick in the night, we headed for the midway. It was here that I had seen the banner for Lionella, so I was given the cultural advantage of not only the opera, but seeing all the great freaks of the day. Eco and Ico, who as freaks had everything going for them. Not only were they twins, they were albinos and their little heads came to a decided point. Even more exotic was their origin-the Gold Coast of Africa! The Great Omi, every inch covered in the most beautiful tattoos you ever laid your eyes on. Daisy and Violet Hilton, Siamese twins who, we were told, had an offer to be separated, but they wouldn't hear of it. They said, "Whom God has joined together, let no man put asunder." When they retired, they went to work at the Piggly Wiggly. One was the checker, the other sacked.

The most fascinating was the Texas Four-Legged Woman. She had two normal legs, but in between she had two little legs. Renata said, "What do you suppose it costs to keep her shod?" She not only had four legs, she was blessed with two female orifices. "Just like a possum," Renata whispered. Because she claimed to have given birth out of both, I asked Renata if that meant her kids were half brothers and sisters. She said she didn't think so, but it may have made her husband a bigamist or an adulterer. Renata told me she'd read in a medical magazine in the dentist's office about a woman who had seventeen nipples. When I told my grandmother she said, "An uneven number. Now, that's not normal."

Renata had a goofy looking boyfriend named Z.T. Willard who worked in the stock room at Leeds Shoe Store. Ever so much time was spent conjecturing what the "Z" stood for. He was from Port Aransas, Texas, and was always after her to marry him and go back there and live with his family. He told her, "You'll just love Mama." But she turned him down flat, and it wasn't because he wanted her to live with his family, but because of her hair. "The gulf is so muggy," she said, "I'd have to shave my head."

I don't know what ever became of her, but whenever I see a fuzzy-haired redhead I cannot help but remember Renata.

✳   ✳   ✳

Not content with taking pictures of family and pets, my family took pictures of neighbors and their pets. One is of a very pretty girl lifting her skirt mid-thigh, head thrown back, saucy. Gazing up at her is a fox terrier. On the back is written, R.S. with Ferdinand."

Living two doors down from us when I was about six years old was an enormously fat couple, Butch and Myrtle Stuber, their two children, Little Butch and Rosemary, and their boarder, Paddy. Mr. Stuber worked the day shift at the slaughterhouse down at the stockyards, and Paddy worked the night shift. Papa said it was obvious which kid was Mr. Stuber's and which was Paddy's because Little Butch was a fat, pink, sweaty kid with tiny eyes who loved to hit people. Mr. Stuber doted on him. Rosemary was thin and attractive, like Paddy.

Mama said the thing that typified the Stubers was that they had a pair of bookends end to end with nothing in between, not even a Reader's Digest. Mama didn't care much for them or their living arrangement and wanted me to stay away from them, but I found the whole setup irresistible; for one thing, Mrs. Stuber would let me play dress-up in all her jewelry. For another, the wallpaper in her kitchen had peas and carrots on it and Mrs. Stuber, to my endless delight, would pretend she was picking them off the wall and eating them.

Paddy would sit on the side porch and tell me that the grease stain on the floor of the garage held an opening to a cave where tiny people, called leprechauns, lived and guarded a treasure. I thought he meant leper cons — dwarf leper convicts guarding all the loot they'd stolen. I was fascinated and wild to see them; Paddy said only special people could see them, but maybe someday I'd be able to. I just hoped it would happen before the cops spotted them.

I asked Mama why the Stubers ate fish on Friday. In Oklahoma, nobody ate fish. Mama said it was because they were Catholics. This word was never said out loud, always *sotto voce*. Sometimes not even that, only mouthed, accompanied by a certain look.

Rosemary would sometimes let me watch her dress for a date. The ritual of her toilette was as elaborate and ordered as Marie Antoinette's. First, she would emerge from the bathroom in a cloud of steam and Cashmere Bouquet talcum powder wearing a peach-colored rayon tricot wrapper (real crawly material) cut on the bias, her hair in Kiddy Curlers. When she was seated on a low stool at her dressing table, the ritual commenced. This dressing table was a fabulous piece of furniture. Very glamorous, unlike Mama's, which just had a chintz flowered skirt around it and a dinky stand-up mahogany mirror. Rosemary's was Hollywood blonde with a matching bench, a high full-length mirror, tiny curved legs, and a space where her knees fit with small drawers on either side for her makeup. I was not her only audience. Rosemary had a fox terrier named Ferdinand, who wore a red harness. None of our dogs even wore collars.

First, with a marabou puff Rosemary patted very pale pink Richard Hudnut powder over her face and neck. She applied Coty rouge with a tiny puff from a small, round tin box. It was a bright fuschia, a gorgeous color in the box. Not so on the cheeks and not only because of its unnatural color, but mostly due to Rosemary's application. Nobody had ever heard of blending. What happened next was the most fascinating. Rosemary took a small, cruel looking instrument with little scissor handles, leaned in very close to the mirror, and ever so carefully clamped it onto her eyelash and squeezed. She called this instrument of torture an eyelash curler. She then slid open the lid of a small red box and spit on her cake mascara, applying it over and over again to her lashes with a tiny brush. This required enormous concentration, and Rosemary's open mouth was pulled way down at the corners. Her eyebrows she plucked to Jean Harlow skinniness. She put her eyebrow pencil in her mouth, clamped her lips around it, gave it a whirl, and painted a thin line over what eyebrows she had left. Next, orange lipstick; she thought it went well with her strawberry blonde coloring. She opened her mouth wide and tight and oh so carefully spread the lipstick on just slightly above her natural lipline, checking to see if she had gotten any on her teeth, then blotting it with a piece of toilet paper. She took the Kiddy Curlers out of her hair and fluffed it out with a big-toothed comb. Pulling on her stockings and twisting around to fasten them to her supporters and getting the seams straight made her break into a sweat, sometimes causing her makeup to run. I guess it never occurred to her to reverse the order and put on the stockings first. She'd squeak, "Sweet Jesus!" and Mrs. Stuber would holler in from the kitchen, "I heard that, sister." I never understood why Mrs. Stuber sounded irritated, because I thought Rosemary was offering up a mini-prayer, her being Catholic and all.

She then stepped into her shoes, which were a wonder—very high heels with snubbed toes called Baby Dolls. She sprayed on perfume, Evening in Paris or Taboo.

Throwing a scarf over her face to keep her makeup from getting smudged, Rosemary pulled a flowered, ruffledy, pongee dress over her head, took off the scarf, checked her makeup again, fluffed out her hair, twirled around in front of the mirror, and struck a Varga girl pin-up pose for Ferdinand and me. A living doll! Both of us were mesmerized, Ferdinand jumping and walking on his hind legs and yapping in a frenzy of excitement. Rosemary said, "Oh, shut up."

She pushed a pile of Bakolite bracelets on her wrists and grabbed up her flat, clutch pocketbook, tucking it under her arm. She pranced out of the house, the screen door slamming behind her, off to catch the streetcar for another evening of swing dancing to Bob Wills and His Texas Playboys down at the Trianon Ballroom.

But, alas, the Stubers did not meet with a happy fate. Used to making the same daily drive to the slaughterhouse for years, delivering Paddy for the night shift, and picking up Mr. Stuber from the day shift, neither Mr. or Mrs. Stuber saw or heard the freight train.

As for Rosemary, six months earlier she had eloped with a young man who ran the Tilt-A-Whirl with a carnival. She took only a shoebox full of makeup and Ferdinand.

Mama was horrified, saying how Rosemary, at fifteen, had "destroyed her future and would never get to complete her education." Papa said, "Don't worry about it, Pauline, it was either that or the streets." Mama said she never thought of it quite that way before.

MY MATERNAL GRANDPARENTS

*　　*　　*

There was a picture of a young woman gazing at a cat that was nursing a baby rabbit along with a litter of kittens. the woman's face was disfigured. My maternal grandmother had told me that in the early part of the twentieth century Orphan Trains had rolled out across the Great Plains of the west and southwest loaded with pitiable human cargo, children from the choked poverty and disease-ridden slums of the Eastern Seaboard. The trains would stop at small watering stations and the children would be rousted out, often in the dead of night, to be examined by farmers who would take them to work as hands. It was much like a horse auction where they were poked and handled to check if they were sound in wind and limb.

One of these children came to live with our family because they heard she had been horribly mistreated by the people who had taken her. Like something out of a Dickens' novel, her only bed had been a pile of rags in a lean-to. While cleaning out the coal scuttle in the kitchen, her dress caught fire and she had been badly burned. My grandmother, hearing that the family now treated her even worse since she was useless to them, sent the buggy for her and nursed her to health. Her name was Annie. And she hated it. She wanted to be called Geraldine. But, like Little Orphan Annie, her lot in life was to:

> Wash the cups and saucers up
> And brush the crumbs away
> And shoo the chickens off the porch
> And dust the hearth and sweep
> And make the fire and bake the bread
> And earn her board and keep.

But my family treated her as one of their own children. She attended all Christmas dinners and Fourth of July picnics, and sat with the family at church, weddings, and funerals. They were prepared to take care of her always, fearing that due to her disfigurement from the burns she would never marry.

But lo and behold, a brakeman for the Frisco Railroad began to court her, or try to. To everyone's surprise and distress, she would have nothing to do with him. Still he pressed his suit. For over a year, Annie rejected him. Then suddenly she announced she'd accepted his marriage proposal. He came to my grandfather and asked to marry Annie, properly.

She was married in my grandmother's parlor, in front of her big bay window. After the reception and before leaving with her brakeman bridegroom, Annie called my grandmother into the butler's pantry. She said she had something to show her that he had given her. From inside the front of her dress, she pulled out a heart-shaped locket. Engraved across the front of it was the name "Geraldine."

✳   ✳   ✳

There was a snapshot of an odd looking character in front of Papa's office with a three-legged dog. This was Tilly Mootz and the three-legged dog was Tripod. Papa said Tripod had made the most of his infirmity; he used it to his distinct advantage—he never had to lift his leg at a fire hydrant. Tilly was an auctioneer and dressed in mismatched clothing he'd scavenged from his auctions. Papa had gotten him out of some minor scrape for which he was eternally grateful.

Papa considered him a natural philosopher of sorts because of his expressions and found him endlessly amusing. Tilly and Tripod would appear at his office every morning to announce the weather report. Some days it was "so dry the trees were bribing the dogs." Other times it was "cold as my ex-wife's heart." In summer it was "hot as a two-dollar whore on the Fourth of July." He'd speak in what he thought were legal terms. "Lawyer Edwards, I have information concerning whereas, if and but and to."

He was filled with jokes: The doctor asked the old woman if she had ever been bedridden. She replied, "Oh yes, doctor, hundreds of times, and twice in a buggy."

He'd married a grass widow and claimed it was because he had foolishly entered into "the most dangerous job alive—drying a widow's tears." In her family was "so rich they could eat their laying hens and put on more airs than an Episcopalian." Whereas his people were "poor as sawmill rats. As a boy I ate so many armadillos, I still roll up into a ball whenever I hear a dog bark."

He allowed as how he had a brother-in-law who was "so ugly when he was born his folks had to borrow a baby to take to the church." Tilly philosophized that "the love of a woman is as the dew of heaven—just as likely to fall on a turd as a rose."

Tilly had a worthless stepdaughter who was insulated from good sense. He called her Radio Station because "anyone can pick her up, especially at night." Once when she served him a plate of collard greens, he found a hair. He told her, "Henceforth, daughter, if you don't mind, I would prefer to have the collards and the hair served separately."

He was originally from Conway, Arkansas, where he eventually retired, despite his belief that "the Baptists and the Johnson grass have taken over." Papa said Tilly's decampment to his native state was the only cultural gain Arkansas had ever made over Oklahoma.

October 10, 1978

Dear Sophronia Gertrude,

Your Mama, I worry, is bereft of reason. She has found a beauty operator who has had her teeth pulled. Now, please try to understand your mother's reasoning. She says that the beauty operator has gone to some tooth carpenter who is going to make her a set of teeth. Your mother is going to wait and see if the beauty operator's teeth fit, and if they do, she is going to the same tooth carpenter. I wish you would please try and figure this one out. I have explained it to several psychiatrists who rejected my money and flatly refused to make any attempt to explain it.

If you can, please wire me collect. I await your assessment of the situation.

I am, as ever, your Paw, W.H.E.

LOT 108

THE CURSE OF THE GYPSY BLOOD

ATENCIÓN GRINGO

For GOLD & GLORY

Come South of
the Border and

Ride

With PANCHO VILLA

El Liberator of Mexico!

WEEKLY PAYMENTS IN GOLD TO
DYNAMITERS ♦ MACHINE GUNNERS ♦ RAILROADERS

Enlistments Taken In Juarez, Mexico
♦ January 1915 ♦

VIVA VILLA! VIVA la Revolución!

he thing looked horrible. It was worn bare and shedding, so I put it outside. It was humpbacked and bound with leather straps. This was my Uncle Homer's hide-covered trunk, so drab that it was a surprise when I opened it and saw pasted on the lid garish cigar box prints of Floradora girls.

The tray was crammed with Mexican newspapers, a ledger marked Stud Book, medicine show handbills, a tearsheet announcing a William Jennings Bryan rally, and a doll-sized sombrero and drum. In the trunk was a stuffed armadillo with a broken tail and its sawdust spilling out, a pair of crossed carbines, an empty bottle of paregoric, a tin cartridge box filled with snake rattles, Mexican spurs with large rowels, leather leggings, a hair bridle, and three rawhide quirts, their tips shredded to ribbons and stiff with dried blood. Some horse must have been ridden hell for leather.

Out of the folds of a saddle blanket fell a crumpled flyer. "ATTENCION Gringo! For GOLD and GLORY, Come south of the border, Ride with PANCHO VILLA, El Liberator of Mexico, weekly payments in GOLD! to Dynamiters . . . Machine Gunners . . . Railroaders!! Enlistments taken in Juarez, Old Mexico. VIVA VILLA! VIVA LA REVOLUCION!!!"

UNCLE HOMER

Uncle Homer was a restless roustabout, a desperado for excitement, forever seeking his own El Dorado. He was a member of that:

> Race of men who don't fit in,
> A race that can't stay still;
> So they can break the hearts of kith and kin,
> And they roam the world at will.
> They range the fields and they rove the flood,
> And they climb the mountain's crest;
> Theirs is the curse of the gypsy blood,
> And they don't know how to rest.

I grew up hearing about his exploits from Papa and my grandfather. The family referred to Homer as Houdini because he had the ability to extricate himself from all manner of complicated schemes of his own making, his usual method being flight. He could be solitary as a snake, simply vanish, not to be heard from for years. They allowed as how he was as daring as the first man who ever ate an oyster.

Once when my grandfather was down in Laredo, Texas, he saw a man sitting on a curb eating hot tamales out of a tin bucket. He approached him and asked, "Aren't you Homer Edwards?" The man looked up and said, "I'm Homer Edwards, but who the hell are you?" My grandfather said, "Well, I'll be damned! I'm your brother, Will. I haven't seen you in twenty years. Where have you been?" Homer said, "I been down in Old Mexico fightin' with Villa," and he offered him a hot tamale.

Papa said, "Homer took up with a gotch eyed off breed woman named Chico Mico, 'little monkey,' on account of her being no bigger than a wart, ugly enough to turn a funeral up an alley and mean as a Mississippi sheriff. He felt beholden to her because she'd driven him to drink and he was grateful to her for it. She ran off and he went hunting her. He found her in a Matamoros jail. She was only in for murder and a little whoring on the side. How she had any customers looking like a little monkey is anyone's guess. Maybe it was because she could do more tricks than a monkey on a trapeze. She'd been thrown into dungeon vile on account of her stabbing one of her customers with a *cuchilla de monte*—a hunting knife—cut him three ways: long, deep, and repeatedly. He lay there bleeding to death for a good long spell before she sent for the policia. Claimed it was a suicide. Chico Mico wasn't just short in the looks department. When they passed out the brains, she didn't hold out her plate. It doesn't take a genius to know that any young man with a pint of tequila in one hand, a sack of corn tamales in the other in a whorehouse on a Saturday night is not going to kill himself. He had everything to live for."

Homer realized the futility of his relationship with Chico Mico. To assuage his grief, he gave a Chiapas Indian a deck of marked cards and a pair of loaded dice for a real monkey which he named Juan. When Homer left the monkey alone in his room, it destroyed everything in it. Once Homer returned to find it laid out flat and glassy eyed. Fearing that the monkey had croaked, his grief knew no bounds, so close it was to the loss of Chico Mico. But when the creature hiccuped, he realized it was dead drunk, having imbibed half a quart of whiskey. Another time, it got sick all over the room from dipping snuff. Juan was turning into a regular juvenile delinquent. Homer tried everything to tempt him into tameness. The little character was scary bright and after observing Homer a couple of times, he learned to roll cigarettes. This accomplishment seemed to soothe and civilize him slightly.

When Homer hired on as a cow puncher on a big south Texas ranch, Juan commenced driving all the cowboys, maids, cats, dogs, horses, and longhorns crazed with his ceaseless torments. Like all monkeys, he was without inhibitions; hence, shockingly obscene. There was no telling when or where he would strike next. He was indiscriminant about what he did or who he did it in front of, having no more respect for the preacher than he did for one of the dogs. He couldn't be contained because he shrieked and tore things apart. So this spoiled child was given the run of the ranch to roam freely, far and wide.

THE STAR JUAN

Juan had the makings of a true arsonist. One of his favorite tricks was to climb up into the barn rafters with a cigarette and a box of Diamond kitchen matches. He enjoyed tobacco in all forms, except for snuff. He savored a good chew of Mail Pouch occasionally, which Homer encouraged, since it was fire free.

Juan was one hell of a bronc rider. But his favorite pastime was to swing from one of the steer's longhorns to the other or hang from his tail while the steer pawed up the earth, bawling at the top of his lungs, wall-eyed with terror.

Papa said, "The turning point in Juan's life came when he discovered love, for someone other than himself, that is." The cook, Annuncia, was hardly the type you'd think Juan would go for, being deeply religious and tending toward flesh, but fall in love he did, and passionately. He gave up tormenting the longhorns and focused all his energies on getting Annuncia's attention. He would hide behind doors and jump out at her, climb on top of cabinets and drop on her from above. But his favorite trick was to take a running leap, grab onto her full skirt or her long braid, and swing. These attacks were performed in a state of very obvious romantic ardor, causing Annuncia to throw her apron over her head and scream, "Chango! Christo! Dios!"

The help threatened to quit, the dogs slunk around with their tails between their legs hunting cover, the cats refused to come out from under the house, and the cattle stampeded. Some action had to be taken. The foreman told Homer it was either his job or Juan. Homer was heartsick, but he put Juan up for adoption. He was rejected by two families in less than an hour. They wanted a monkey who didn't smoke. A small zoo agreed to take him. He was placed in a monkey cage. His adjustment was poor. He missed a good smoke, the longhorns, and Annuncia.

Homer couldn't bear to see Juan pine so. He asked the zoo to give him back, which they were more than happy to do. When next the family heard from him he had hit the road again and tied up with a medicine show hawking Grove's Tasteless Chill Tonic, a product heavily laced with dope.

The show was run by a Madame Adam, a bearded, fire-eating dwarf. Together, they traveled all over the south and southwest. Juan turned out to be an enormous asset. The medicine show crowds loved him and his cigarette routine. Once he got the smell of the sawdust and the roar of the crowd in him, his talents expanded. Homer could teach him a trick overnight, but Juan created the best tricks from his own fertile imagination. He could walk a clothesline while balancing an umbrella, play a tambourine, beat the drum, and perform the Mexican hat dance.

My grandfather told me, "While in Duval Coun-

ty, Texas, Homer ran on to a Mexican who was looking to sell his flea circus. The fleas' host cat kept
turning out litters of eight-toed hairless kittens, and
the fleas had been thrown off their feed by the trau-
ma of no place to hide and exposure to light. They
were starving. The Mexican figured he could do as
well exhibiting the cats as the fleas, and they were a
lot easier to keep track of. So Homer watered down
a case of Grove's Tasteless Chill Tonic and traded it
for the anemic fleas."

Madame Adam was not overly fond of Juan, being
jealous of his diminutiveness as well as his obvious
pronounced gender. Juan, in turn, hated the fleas;
he knew they had replaced him as the star attraction.
Having been a headliner, he refused to share the bill
with them, which was just as well. Being a monkey,
he had an innate ability for grooming, which was
death on fleas. Once he was at liberty, he spent his
days lounging around smoking.

Billed as "The Tiny Mights," (Homer refused to
allow their names to be spelled m-i-t-e-s because the
fleas were as insulted by that as being called lice),
they drew record crowds.

Homer called himself Professor Pules Irritans,
after the scientific name of the species hosted by
humans. He began his spiel with a quote from a
medieval poem:

> "Ah, the flea, born to range the merry world,
> To rob at will the veins delectable of princes
> To lie with ladies, Ah, fairest joy!"

Homer claimed he never met a dull flea.

In his lecture prior to the act, he said, "Ladies and gentlemen, step right up. May the members of the audience wearing spectacles, please, be allowed the courtesy of the front. For your edification and enjoyment, Caesar and Cleopatra, our stars, accompanied by the entire troupe, will perform, in unison, a flying leap over the equivalent of London's Saint Paul's Cathedral, and they will do it not once, but six hundred times in an hour, if need be, for three days in a row! Trivial, their grandson, possesses the fastest single switch mechanism of any organism. He is also the proud owner of the most elaborate set of genitalia in the animal kingdom. Hence, proportionately, enjoys a complex and active love life. With prodigious energy, you will observe him lift off at one hundred and forty times the force of gravity, and soar to an apogee of ten inches. I must request, ladies and gentlemen, that those closest to the stage please refrain from coughing or sneezing. Thank you for your courtesy to the artists. Caesar! Let the games begin!"

Homer sold cards, "For Gents Only," with a drawing of "The Merry Flea . . . whose reproductive parts occupy one third of his body length while in repose and come equipped with Spines, Lopes, Tickling Devices for the Lucky Missus! This Amazing Appendage takes a meandering route of often wrong turns, entering taking ten minutes and oft lasting three to nine hours!"

"Marke but this flea, and marke in this
It sucked me first and now sucks thee
And in this flea our two bloods mingled be,
John Dunne.'

Homer was always having to corral the fleas out of Madame Adam's beard until she commenced squirting it with citronella. But calamity hit in Pine Bluff, Arkansas, when, hung over from the night before, Madame Adam became careless during her fire-swallowing act and her beard caught fire. She was thrown into a nearby horse trough, but it was too late. Not just for her beard, which had been singed beyond recall, but some of the fleas perished in the fire as well, thereby depleting the herd.

As is so often the case, show business and politics commingled. Homer had barely been able to eke out a living until that fateful day when, on a campaign swing through the southwest, William Jennings Bryan caught the act. He immediately sensed the fleas' political potential. He put Homer on a retainer and signed the fleas to an exclusive contract. New costumes were designed, the better to draw crowds before his political rallies.

So Homer bid Madame Adam (who was beginning to sprout a scrofulous beard) a fond farewell, packed up his livestock, and hit the campaign trail.

He created a new act in preparation for election day. The climax came when the whole troupe, like a twenty-mule team of atomies, pulled a walnut shell chariot topped by a flag which read "Vote for William Jennings Bryan." When Bryan saw it in dress rehearsal, he feared it might even surpass his Cross of Gold speech.

As election day approached, Caesar began sitting down on the job, and it spread like wildfire throughout the troupe. They were filled with ennui. Since Homer's livelihood depended on the fleas, he was in a state of nervous prostration. He could have sympathized had it been a matter of temperament, as the little buggers were overworked the closer it came to opening the show. He thought, "Maybe the little blood suckers are off their feed." Recently, some country boob had referred to Caesar as "a louse." He knew it had hurt and offended him. He always knew when something was troubling Caesar because the height of his jumps was off and he refused to breed for protracted periods. He'd not touched Cleopatra for weeks, which affected her performance as well, undermining her confidence and self-esteem.

Disaster struck when the fleas in costume were waiting in the wings. When their music started they refused to enter. The cue was played again and still they refused. Homer was apoplectic with rage at the little moochers. He began threatening them, hoping to throw the fear of God and a strong wind into them. They remained immobile.

Homer knew "the fate of a nation was riding that night." When William Jennings Bryan lost, Homer took it as a personal tragedy. His fleas had altered the outcome of the election and forever changed the course of history.

Homer wired the Mexican that he'd sell the fleas

back to him cheap, but the Mexican wired back he couldn't use them because he was doing so well with the cats, who were still turning out hairless litters.

Despite their betrayal, Homer couldn't find it in his heart to put them down, no matter how painless. They had provided him with good years of income and companionship. He released them all on to a passing bloodhound, not wanting to break up the family. The mystery of their mutiny was never solved. Homer always suspected it was because they were Republicans.

My grandfather heard the entire catastrophic experience disillusioned and saddened Homer, and that he sought to lift his spirits by a change of scene. Juan was ecstatic to be rid of his rivals, the fleas, and looked forward to new horizons as well. Homer saw an ad in an Everglade, Florida newspaper. "Reptile Ranch! Start Your Own Business! Fun For the Whole Family!" This sounded less precarious than the theater, so he and Juan traveled south and met the owner, Bo "Gater" Gaines. He had begun his career as a footwashing Baptist preacher until, as he explained, the call of the wild was louder than the call of the Lord, so he took to raising gaters. "Gaters have been good to me," he told Homer. "They are appreciative critters. You treat them with dignity and respect, never talk down to them, and they will reward you in more ways than you ever thought possible."

Homer thought his asking price seemed steep until Gater Gaines outlined how he came up with his figures. "You stop and think what you are getting for your money. Two thousand linear feet of live alligator, in any configuration desired. You can get two hundred ten-footers, one thousand two-footers, any combination you want; but I strongly advise you take a couple of fifteen-footers, Those are the big draw, the ones people really want to see." He said he'd throw in the alligator wrestling lessons free, but Homer rejected that offer, telling Gater Gaines that he wasn't interested in that much hands-on closeness with his employees.

Gater Gaines' reptile wranglers were recovering drunks so he claimed that the gator truly had been an animal of salvation. He urged Homer to buy the business quickly, before someone else "snapped it up."

Homer figured if it was his lot in life to deal with reptiles, better gators who attacked from the front, head on, than the snakes in show business and politics who struck from behind when his back was turned. Although it was a new species of livestock, he enjoyed the grooming and feeding of the alligators. He even gave them names, and when he called them, they came to him. This touched and flattered him.

Papa said, "Juan felt safe and at home in this tropical climate. It put him in the mind of his boyhood in Old Mexico." He even gave up smoking, preferring to hurl bananas and coconuts at the sluggish gators from his treetop perches. Juan had always been a great one for conversation, and now he chattered incessantly, happy and content.

Just as the tourist season was at its height, a hurricane blew in, striking the reptile ranch with such violence that it lashed the cages, scattered the egg nests, and uprooted Juan's trees. It even flung the fifteen-footers over the house. Flying gators filled the air. When after five days the storm played itself out, nothing was left but a swamp where the only living things were the water moccasins.

In despair over his bad fortune, Homer roamed up into the Indian Nation where he thru in with Pawnee Bill's Wild West Show. They had heard about Homer's skill with horses so they hired him on as a hand. Pawnee Bill had taken it into his head that he wanted to breed a striped mule to pull the show wagons with. Homer hit on the notion to breed a jack donkey with a mare zebra. They took to each other and it took. My grandfather said, "The result that emanated from that coupling was the damndest equine I ever laid eyes on. It couldn't be blamed on God because God had better sense. Even if He had thought it up late on the sixth day, He'd have left it off when He loaded the ark. The creature was horrible to look at and mean, with the stubbornness of a donkey and the wildness of a zebra, but Pawnee was so pleased with this useful pet that he couldn't get enough of them. The jack and the zebra obliged, and in no time they had a herd of these 'zules,' as Homer called them.

"The mule will work for you for ten years for the privilege of kicking you once. And the mule (from the Greek root mulas) is sterile, so it can't reproduce itself. It has no pride of ancestry or hope of posterity. This frustrated Homer, and he was bound and determined to alter the injustice nature had imposed on the mule/zule—as every man wants to leave some accomplishment behind him. He knew that with his talent and acumen he could do better. He had tenacity and commitment, and damned if it didn't pay off. He hatched a colt that was a stallion! He called him Blue Moon because he was so rare."

Blue Moon and Juan were stablemates and the fastest of friends. Juan, wearing purple and gold racing silks, mounted on Blue Moon during the Grand Entry, circled the arena at breakneck speed twice a day and three times on Saturday. Homer knew they were a triumvirate the likes of which heretofore the world had never seen, and their future was boundless. Papa said, "They became famous all across the country, and the show made a fortune exhibiting them. Blue Moon was to Pawnee Bill's Wild West Show what Gargantua was to Ringling Brothers. But Blue Moon couldn't take the pressure and the responsibility of knowing that he was the first and possibly the last of a new species. He went so loco they had to geld him. It broke Homer's heart, and he and Pawnee split the blanket over it."

Homer felt it would be selfish of him to take Juan away from Blue Moon, the spotlight, and the stardom he had worked so hard for and so justly deserved. They had experienced much together, and Juan had risen from an untamed beast, dependent and delinquent, to a self-supporting sophisticate. He smoked a corncob pipe now. Homer knew Juan had surpassed him and it would be wrong to return him to the vagabond life. When Homer explained it to him, Juan seemed to understand, for he clung to him. He took Homer's face in his tiny hands and looked into his eyes with a beseeching expression. As Homer rode off the lot, Juan's piteous cries echoed in his ears.

Papa said, "Homer drifted, a broken man astride a mare zebra, over to Crown King, Arizona, where he threw in with a tinhorn gambler and a remittance man and they took to mining for gold; but Homer feared his international reputation was destroyed, and he longed for the old days when he was on top. Donkeys were used in the mines, so there were plenty of them around. He hoped to get a repeat of his past success. He died when he was damn near ninety, still trying to create another Blue Moon."

As I closed the trunk lid, a yellowed newspaper clipping caught my eye. "JUAN DIES. The famous monkey, Juan, star of Pawnee Bill's Wild West Show, has died. The cause of death was uncertain. Pawnee Bill announced that he seemed to sadden and pass away from heartbreak."

January 10, 1979

Dear Sophronia,

Your Mama has been enjoying the heat immensely. She complains constantly, which is her usual method of enjoying herself. I procured for her 100 tablets for aging women. She took twelve of them and began to feel better, whereupon she immediately decided they would probably kill her and she then wouldn't have anything to complain about, so she quit taking them. She refuses to take any medicine for fear it might alleviate her suffering. So I'm around to the point where I am beginning to enjoy her suffering with her. I hope she will gain a little weight so she can help me break some horses. Her ill-fitting false teeth are also giving her pleasure.

In order to save money, for fear of wearing the teeth out, she eats without them. This has not improved her disposition. And in the morning without her teeth, I cannot help but think of the famous poem, Upon Seeing A Louse on a Lady's Bonnet in Church by Robert Burns:

*Oh, would that some power the gift give us
To see ourselves as others see us.*

I took your mother for better or worse. The better is all worn out, and I'm stuck with the worse.

I am, as ever, your Paw, W.H.E.

LOT 102

WHAT BECAME OF THEM

hen I opened the box, a strong smell of mothballs escaped. There lay my Classen High School pep club uniform. Bright blue, pleated wool skirt, long-sleeved yellow sweater with a felt comet blazed across the front and "Classen Comets" across the back. Under it were my saddle oxfords. Shaking out my uniform, I thought, "Was I ever that small?"

Stacked in the box were yearbooks. In my class there was Shirley Jennings, a Kathryn Grayson look-alike: black hair, pale skin, small bones, big bosom. In a picture she was wearing her football queen crown and was perched on the shoulder of the team captain. The players were crouched around her in starting positions. There amongst them was Don Ray Langdorfer. My heart hurt, seeing Don Ray like this. His beauty leaped off the page.

The last time I saw Don Ray was at the high school 25th reunion, accompanied by a man who looked like a bouncer. Don Ray's beauty had faded to a shadow and there was a vacant look in his eyes. I learned he had been in an asylum for fifteen years and he'd been brought to the reunion by a male nurse. Later in the evening, I saw him in a corner. He seemed agitated, sweating, and when I next looked, he was gone.

Arnold Fagin's father and Papa had been friends.

Arnold and I traveled to California together on the train to compete in the National Forensic League Finals. I participated in Oral Interpretation of Dramatic Literature, and Arnold, as captain of the debate team, argued "Resolved: Should the U.S. Have Compulsory Military Training?"

A full-page photograph showed Janice Lee Dowling seated on a stage throne as the band queen. She was tall, willowy, lovely, always in love with Jimmy Lee Mackin, the drum major. He was thrown from a horse and crippled. Janice Lee married him anyway.

Donny Domminck appeared in all the school assemblies because he could play the accordion and tap dance. He was small, dark, and pretty as a girl.

Patrica Borella, half Italian-half Irish, with bright red hair and a gorgeous body, our ballet dancer, did not graduate. Instead she left for Hollywood her senior year and danced in movie musicals.

As adorable as a speckled pup, Bibi Rickie was a tiny blonde who nurtured a Betty Grable look. She was the first person I ever saw wear an angora sweater. It was pink, which made her look like cotton candy; delicious. Telltale pieces of fuzz were spotted on boys' athletic sweaters after lunch period; hence, she was thought of as being fast. She married Timmy Lord three days after graduation and seven months later gave birth. If that wasn't shocking enough, Mama said, "She had the gall to have twins!" She named them Heavenly and Precious Lord. We had never known her to be religious.

I had been in grade school with Carolyn Beth

Pyle. She was tall, slender and had large dark brown eyes, olive skin and blush red cheeks. Her mother fascinated me because she was pretty and young and wore bobby socks. She seemed no more than a teenager. Mrs. Pyle's father was a Tishimingo judge and preacher and strict with her, but she foiled him by climbing out a window and eloping. Carolyn Beth was focused, highly motivated and ambitious. She excelled in everything she put her mind to. These qualities appealed to my mother probably because she recognized some of herself in Carolyn Beth. By grade school Carolyn Beth was an accomplished pianist, disciplining herself to practice hours every day on an upright piano. Mama wanted to ask her to practice on our Steinway grand but it was always out of tune. Carolyn Beth was offered a musical scholarship but she got married instead. This puzzled and upset Mama. She said, "How uncharacteristic of Carolyn Beth, a girl as gifted and intelligent as she is! *Why?* She could get married *anytime!*" Mama didn't want to admit that a young girl might be motivated by something other than rationality, no matter how bright or talented.

All the money in the world couldn't help the plain daughter of Juanita and Red Hicker, Redrita. Red Hicker became a millionaire as a wildcatter. Redrita was driven to school in a Lincoln Continental with a tire on the back, chauffeured by one of Red's roustabouts on his oil rig. Juanita feared Redrita would be kidnapped and held for ransom like the Lindberg baby. Papa said Juanita was putting in a lot of wasted time worrying because, "The kid favors old Red, who is as homely as homemade sin." Redrita later married the roustabout on the site of Red's first well and the champagne gushed out of a miniature oil derrick. Five years later, Red told Papa, "Me and Juanita are worried sick that Redrita is a dry hole. I told her husband, maybe his bit is too short and to keep drilling." Finally, they had Redrita, Jr.

I started to turn the page of the yearbook when a picture of a girl in the lower corner stopped me. Her chin was tucked down shyly, but her eyes were looking straight into the camera. Her name was Frankie Faye Brown. She was of average height, with long, dark, naturally curly hair. She had a wide, sensual mouth and wore bright red lipstick. Her figure was full and perfectly proportioned. Something about her fascinated me. I had not only wanted to know her, I wanted to know all about her, but she was elusive. Between classes, she walked close to the lockers in the hallways, her head down, as if she didn't want to be noticed.

In music class, it was apparent that Frankie Faye had a lovely voice. I was determined to meet her, so I told her how good I thought her voice was. Softly, she said, "I can dance, too."

I helped plan the assembly programs and asked her if she would participate. To my surprise, she accepted eagerly. She stepped on the stage in her saddle oxfords, bobby sox, sweater and skirt, threw her weight on one leg, and sang:

Oh, my man, I love you so . . .

She flung her arms above her head and began to dance. A real little high school Gilda. The teachers were none too pleased. The students applauded wildly. She had to do an encore.

I've got you under my skin . . .

I became a friend and champion of Frankie Faye. I discovered she lived in a tiny house, set on a dirt lot where no lawn would grow. One time at school I found her in the girls' washroom in a stall, crouched down, racked with sobs. And then, as suddenly as she appeared, she disappeared.

Ten years later, the stage manager came backstage at a theatre where I was working in Dallas. He said I had a visitor. There stood Frankie Faye, beautiful and still shy. She said she had become an exotic dancer and asked if I would come to see her. I told her of course I would. After my performance one night, I took a cab to a downtown striptease club.

When Frankie Faye was announced, the trumpet player stood up. He started to play "Whispering." Suddenly, as if by magic, Frankie Faye appeared. She was barefooted and wore a pale, diaphanous cloak that wafted about her. The place fell silent. Even the drunks stopped talking. There were no bumps, no grinds, just floating. She had an innate, sweet sexuality. She performed only for the trumpet player. They never took their eyes off each other.

She dropped her cloak and stood before us, her entire skin shimmering with iridescent sequins. She put her hands on both breasts, then kissed her palms and blew those kisses to her trumpet player. And then, she was gone.

Frankie Faye had graced the place with her innocence. She was released from the bondage of her shyness by her talent, which gave her the ability to be emotionally exposed and vulnerable publicly.

I hope her trumpet player was good to her and stayed in love with her. Frankie Faye deserved that.

✻   ✻   ✻

Alongside the yearbook there was a musical jewel box with a ballerina on the lid that must have, at some time, twirled when opened. Inside, among the medals for speech contests, was a charm bracelet of European coins. I had gotten them when I went to Europe with my maternal grandmother after graduation. Both of us traveled on her passport.

Everyone needs time away from a traveling companion, even more so at 16. Especially a chaperone. My grandmother, like any sensible person when in Spain, took an afternoon siesta. I took advantage of this one afternoon in Seville and escaped. I wandered into a cathedral to avoid the sweltering heat. When I came out I saw him. He was sucking a blood orange. He threw it at a pigeon and approached me as if he had been waiting for me. He looked to be about 12, hard muscled as an adult, with a pretty, sticky face. His rough little hands were covered in scratches. He stood directly in my path and grinned teasing, overly familiar, like an imp, beckoning me to come with him. When I tried to go around him, he boldly took my hand. I pulled away and he expressed mock apologies and did a cartwheel, graceful as an acrobat.

I headed for the shady side of the street. The shopkeepers were lifting the grates to open their stores after the afternoon siesta. The boy followed, whistling softly in an odd, minor key, and occasionally calling out, "Que pasa?" to the shopkeepers, who all seemed to know him. I stopped to look in a window and when I moved away, there he was in front of me again. This time walking backwards, pantomiming sweeping a path for me. Then he dashed away. As I rounded the corner, an arm shot out from behind a column. Like one of the rude characters out of *commedia dell'arte*, a crooked finger beckoned, "Psst." Hoping to escape him, I went into a shop. When I came out, I was relieved to see he was gone. But that was too much to hope for because I heard him calling, "Señorita! Señorita!" I looked back to see him running toward me, waving my shawl which I had left in the store. I tried to tip him, hoping he would go away, but he would have none of it.

Emboldened by finally making contact with me, he commandeered my sack of souvenirs with the authority of a liveried chauffeur. He somehow completely took over, and I let him. He beckoned me to "Come, come." I don't know why I followed him. Perhaps because I had seen all the sights in Seville, had no plans for the evening, and was leaving the next day.

We seemed to walk forever through winding, narrow streets. He had an innate sense of when I was beginning to tire and led me to a bench by a fountain to rest for a few minutes. He crouched on his heels at my feet, fanning me with a newspaper and making sympathetic noises. We continued on down a narrow, dark set of steps and came out into an open space teeming with activity. Scattered about were small, tattered tents and one large tent. I realized we were on the back lot of a circus.

He led me past the ticket takers and made a great show of getting me a special seat. It was only one ring. The band was excellent, the aerialists superb, and the equestrians some of the best I'd ever seen.

Suddenly there were flashes of heat lightening and all the lights went out. The audience sat patiently, as if this were a common occurrence. In the darkened tent, a clown stood behind each couple with children, while my guide took their picture to sell them at the end of the show. A very clever piece of marketing, I thought. What parent does not want a picture of their child with a clown?

I realized, once I was not distracted by the show, that it was stifling inside the tent. I got up to get some air. From nowhere, my guide was at my elbow. He beckoned me to follow him. As we walked toward an odd makeshift structure, I smelled a strong, unpleasant odor. He pulled back a piece of tattered canvas and proudly announced, "Hippopotamum!"

And there it stood, in a tank of water. I was amazed that any tiny circus would travel with such an ungainly beast and one that was so difficult to care for, as it had to spend portions of every day submerged in water. He was delighted by my amazement.

The lights had come back on, so he took me back to my seat and got me a drink of orange juice. The band started to play a waltz, and an elegant couple— the man in tails and the woman in a flowing, beaded caftan—entered the arena. He blindfolded her and then pickpocketed articles from members of the audience; glasses, a watch, handkerchiefs and keys. He then would ask the woman what he was holding and she would tell him exactly what it was.

After the final march of all the performers around the ring, my guide once again materialized. I thanked him, tried to tip him, and again he refused my offer. I tried to extricate myself to return to my hotel, but he protested, indicating that the evening was not yet over. I could not imagine what he had in store that could top a circus. Or the "hippopotamum."

He led me off the lot, which already seemed to show almost no signs of anyone having been there, as the circus had "folded its tents like the Arabs" and disappeared.

Again we walked a considerable way, and I saw a bonfire glowing in the darkness. I heard the strange, minor singing wail and hand clapping of a gypsy camp. People were laughing, drinking, milling around. Dogs ran loose barking. Just outside the glow of the fire, a man played a guitar. I recognized the tune as the same one the boy had whistled. And in the light of the fire a woman was dancing in a ruffled polka-dot dress. I could see that she was very pregnant, but it in no way impeded her graceful, seductive movements. In fact, it enhanced her sexuality. As my guide pulled me in close by the fire, I thought the guitar player and the woman looked familiar. "Mi madre, mi padre," the boy said, gesturing toward them. And then I recognized them from the circus as the man in tails and the blindfolded woman in the caftan. My guide leapt up and began to dance with skill and passion. He was brutally masculine beyond his years.

We stayed late, and then he led me back to my hotel. He became more adamant in his refusal when I started to reach in my purse to tip him. I rang for the concierge, and when I looked up he was gone.

My grandmother demanded an explanation and I told her the whole story. I fell into bed exhausted and slept late. When we checked out, I couldn't find my wallet. I went back to the room to look for it, then realized that in my exhaustion, I had not noticed that my watch and both bracelets, plus my class ring, were gone. Then it hit me. I had been a victim of an Artful Dodger. But when had it happened? When he first took my hand? In the tent with the hippo? When the lights had gone out? At the gypsy camp?

Like good, law-abiding American citizens, we had the concierge notify the police. I led them to the grounds and there were no signs of the circus, the tattered tents, or the "hippopotamum." At the gypsy camp, except for the ashes of a burnt out fire, it was as if I had dreamed it, as if they had never existed, or had been carried off by the wind. And it was then that the realization hit me—I had been "stolen by gypsies!"

My darling daughter Gertie,

I hope you continue to be gainfully employed. It will keep you out of meanness. Whatever part you take it is better than walking and toting a rail, so long as it is clean. I did not see you talking to this Johnny Carson, whoever he is. Word has it you are meeting with some success. Just remember not to take up with any scrub cattle. I have found, from years of observation, that you can get all the friends in the world, as long as you furnish the whiskey.

Your mama went back to the tooth carpenter. He put in an hour wrestling her false teeth. She is convinced they don't work, so they repose in the dishwasher or under the dresser or wherever she can find room to throw them down. That way she will have something to complain about the rest of her life. With advancing years, her complaints become more vigorous than they were in our youth. She stands around with a hump in her middle, like an old cow with an early calf. I am going to put an ad in the paper and see if I can get a young widow woman and put up some booty. However, your mama says that, at my age, I would not be able to raise enough boot!

I am, as ever, Your Paw., W.H.E.

LOT 110

Kindness to Crooks

There was a packet of loose papers in a manila envelope marked "OKLAHOMA COUNTY SHERIFF'S DEPARTMENT." They were jail forms and copies of letters with Papa's signature vouching for released prisoners.

"One Eugene White, male Negro. Public drunkenness, July 4, 1939." Same forms, same day, July 4, for the years 1940, 1941, 1942, and 1943. There was a handwritten letter to Papa attached.

Dear Mr. Edwards,
Me and my girls want to thank you for helping Eugene. I tried to raise him right. I took him to Sunday school and church ever week. I don't know how come him to act so bad. He is named after his daddy, who was a good man. He is married to that red savage and her and her ways work on him bad. I want to write and tell you that me and my family is all beholden to you for getting Eugene out of jail again. I wish I could promise you it wouldn't happen again, but I don't want to go to the bad place for lying. Mrs. Eugene White.

Eugene White, a misnomer if there ever was one, was a huge black man who worked for us for years. He was so black, his gums were blue. A scar ran from his temple down across his cheek, nose, and upper

lip, ending on his jaw on the other side of his face—
the result of his wife's attack with a straight razor
when she caught him with another woman. Eugene
said, "Pearl, she always sulled up, like a possum."
Pearl could be scary; never talking much, hawk-
nosed, thin-lipped, light coppery skin. Papa said she
had Indian blood. When she cut Eugene with the
razor, Papa persuaded the sheriff not to press
charges. Pearl told Papa, "Mr. Edwards, Eugene
White is sorry. He ain't fit to carry guts to the buz-
zards."

On days when Pearl wasn't sulled up, I'd beg her
to let me see her East Dallas special, a butcher knife
shaved to a point like an ice pick. She carried it in
her garter. Thrilling!

Papa always spoke very highly of Mrs. White,
Eugene's mother. He said she came from good people. The sheriff would always call Papa along about
midnight, and say, "Warren, we've got Eugene down
here in the drunk tank." Papa would get dressed and
go down and bail him out. Papa never lectured
Eugene or seemed to resent it. That's just the way
things were.

When my baby sister was about three years old she
put her hand on Eugene's arm several times, each
time looking at her palm. Eugene chuckled and said,
"No, peanut, the black don't come off."

Eugene took the pledge over and over until it
finally stuck. He died an old man and sober. Papa
spoke at his funeral.

✳   ✳   ✳

There are two release forms for "Pat Pugh. White, male. Tampering with city property," and "Pat Pugh. White male. Possession of bantam fighting cocks. Taking bets within the city limits."

Papa disapproved of almost everything his friend Pat Pugh did, but at the same time he thought everything he did was funny. They had met at Oklahoma High School when Pat moved from the Mule Capital of the World, Columbia, Tennessee. He spoke with a heavy accent in sonorous, senatorial tones. He said, "I refer to my boy, the fruit of my loins, as Meatball, due to his rotund physiognomy." And he reported, "During the Great War, when the influenza hit the country, I arose before the dawn of each new day to check the obituary column to see if my name was listed." Mama said, "Dorothy Pugh comes from lovely people. Whatever possessed her to marry someone as eccentric as Pat." Dorothy Pugh could have asked the same of Mama.

Pat owned a Ford agency. It was at the top of an incline where the road sloped down under a viaduct. When it rained that low area would flood and fill up with red mud. The city tried to fix it with a new drainage system, engineers studied it, and the sewer manager worked on it, but every year it continued to flood. Pat would send Matt Thomas down with a tow truck and charge $10 to haul the cars out. Pat loved the rainy season. Late one night, he called Papa from jail and said, "Warren, I've had a bit of a misunderstanding with the local gendarmes, who have misinterpreted some of my actions." It seems Pat had been caught *in flagrante delicto*, holding a flashlight and instructing Matt how to dam up the viaduct.

One of the more serious of the jail releases lists, "Matt Thomas, white male, odometer tampering." Clipped to it are papers from the state pen, where he served three years. Matt was 6'4", with heavy, long bones. He carried his false teeth in a snuff sack in his pants pocket. As a result they had cracked, and he'd stuck them together with tar. Rarely did they reside in his mouth. I'd beg him to put them in and take them out so I could watch his face collapse on itself like a tent. Then he'd fill his lip with snuff. When I first saw this routine, I ran to describe it to Mama, who said, "How disgusting!"

Matt had started as a garage mechanic whose specialty was turning odometers back on used cars. But he'd gotten caught stealing a pickup loaded with chickens, with 190,000 miles on it and four bald tires. "Poor Matt," Papa said, "didn't even have the good sense to unload the fryers. With all that squawking, you could hear him coming for 40 miles." Papa plea bargained him down from grand theft auto to stealing chickens.

Matt worked around the house. When the roof of the garage began to leak, he said he'd fix it and it wouldn't cost anything for materials. We were going on a week's vacation and Matt said he'd have it finished by the time we got back. Sure enough, when we drove in Matt was putting on the final touches. He couldn't wait to show Papa. Papa climbed up on a ladder and nearly lost his footing when he beheld, imbedded in tar and covering the entire roof, Oklahoma license plates. When we kids asked where he got them, Mama said, "Don't press." Papa said, "After all, Matt was a car thief. He was only using the tools he knew best. But who would have ever guessed he was artistic?"

*　　*　　*

This letter was addressed to Warren H. Edwards, County Attorney's Office, Oklahoma County Court House, Oklahoma City.

December 31, 1946

To My Esteemed Benefactor of Today and Staunch Friend of Yesteryear:

From August 7th, the day I departed the Okla. County jail, to Dec. 31, is 4 months and 24 days that I have, for one reason or another, neglected to write you, which I so honestly intended to immediately consummate when I left Okla. City. Almost five months is a very short time to one who leads a useful, productive and well-coordinated happy life, but can be a very long time to one who has been beset by trial and tribulation of his own making. But however be that reflection, this letter, though it be delinquent, is primarily to express my most sincere and heartfelt appreciation and sheer gratitude for your unmatched kindness, consideration, integrity and pure compassion for me in a troublesome time of dire need. May I say that in my books you are indeed The Good Samaritan and I shall not forget it ever. I am reminded of a passage of Scripture from the Book of Books: "By their deeds ye shall know them." May it be ever so. I believe my urge to attempt some degree of eloquence in striving to express my genuine estimation of your professional, social and spiritual qualities may be pardoned in the light of considering the fact that the break you gave me is absolutely unprecedented in the thirty years of my turbulent and checkered career. I remember well as do you, the glorious days of the long past in good old Okla. High School, when we were on a common ground and footing. Though fate has decreed a yawning divergence in our respective courses, you along the more or less straight and narrow path of self-discipline to success, I over the broad highway of self-abandonment to the inevitable catastrophe, I am proud to observe that such a situation has not turned your head one whit! That you are your same old self and the dead right sport I used to know.

As this hectic 1946 goes into oblivion, I take this fleeting opportunity to wish for you and yours a world of success, prosperity, longevity, happiness and blessed peace all through the fast approaching New Year of 1947 and for all time thereafter.

I am as ever your boyhood friend,

J. Rannell Warren

On the back of the letter Papa had written "Fate spins the wheel and hands some men the jackpot and others aces and eights—a dead man's hand."

December 2, 1976

Dear Daughter Sophronia,

I want all my children home at Christmas. I am still a child at heart this time of year. Nobody can ever know the joy it has always given me to go through the house early in the morning and see all my children sound asleep in their beds, all well and strong at home, the big Christmas tree, the presents and to know the love we have for each other. I can never forget the first Christmas tree I ever saw. It was a big blackjack tree with leaves still on it. Momma and Aunt Lillie and my Grandma Hamilton and my aunts, Modena, Ruth and Ethyl, had strung popcorn and cranberries all over it and when I woke up Christmas morning there it was, the wonder of the world and the most beautiful thing I ever saw in my life and presents for everybody. Santa Claus had been there in the night. My whole life I have never forgotten that wonderful morning, so from that day until the day of my death, I must have a big tree and the joy of my family around me. Life has been wonderful to your mama and me. Four wonderful, healthy children and healthy grandchildren. None of them can ever know the love I have for them.

I am, as ever, your Paw
W.H.E.

LOT 302

MAMA AND PAPA

MAMA

I tore open the box marked "Mama and Papa."
There were Papa's Stetsons and boots and
Mama's initialed silver mirror, comb, and
hair receiver. The sight and mixed aroma was
too much.

Months later, I knew I had put it off as long as I
could. Farther down in the box was a long, narrow
picture of their Oklahoma High School graduating
class, Mama's Phi Beta Kappa certificate, Papa's law
degree, Mama's wedding portrait, and pictures of
them together on their fiftieth and sixtieth wedding
anniversaries.

Papa, his father and uncles had drilled the first gas well in Montana. There was a loose snapshot of Papa taken in Montana wearing a cap and Levis. His thumb was hooked in his belt, his weight on one foot. On the back was written, "Please don't hate me, my darling, for you see, I love you." What could he have meant? I remember there had always been contention between my folks about Montana, where they had gone to live right after they were married. He had blamed her for their returning to Oklahoma. He always said, "If Pauline would have been willing to stay in Montana, they'd have asked me to sleep between them and their wives. They'd have elected me governor." Mama always corrected him, saying it was his folks that had forced him to come back to Oklahoma. It was never resolved.

Under the pictures was Mama's tattered THE GIRL GRADUATE'S MEMORY BOOK, embossed in gold on the rotted leather cover. The front page read, "This book belongs to Pauline Caroline Mills. Oklahoma High School Graduation, May 29, 1919. Flower: Poppy. Colors: Red and White." The contents were almost unbearably poignant.

Mama's father was a railroad conductor who had moved the family from a tiny town in Missouri to Oklahoma City when she was 15. Being newcomers, they had no social connections, yet she somehow had managed to establish herself both academically and socially. She had a lead in the school play, was on the debate team, participated in many school activities

MAMA ~ PAULINE CAROLINE MILLS AS A GIRL GRADUATE.

and excelled in every one. She won the gold Letzeiser Award, given to the student with the highest grade average.

The comments by her classmates not only reveal much about her and their high regard for her, but about themselves as well.

Dearest Pauline,
Ever since I met you in a little Spanish
class down on A floor, I put you down on my
list as the 'Ace of all Aces' amongst the
dashing beauties of O.H.S. and you sure
top the cake for being studious.

Your friend,
Buck McClain

Dear Pauline,
Here's looking at the winner of the
Letzeiser medal. May many honors come to
you in the future.

Dixie Gilmer
(He became county attorney in Tulsa.)

My dear Pauline,
May you always be such a dear friend of
Dame Fortune that you may never meet with
that incorrigible daughter of hers, Mis-Fortune.

Bernice Edwards
(Papa's sister.)

These comments go on page after page, effusive in their respect for her accomplishments, her friendliness, and her beauty. They were more than matched by the comments from her teachers. She was a golden girl.

There were pages with pieces of fabric and notes telling where they were worn. "Commencement—White lace; Junior Senior Reception—Peach georgette, over pink, blue sash, black lace hat, black satin oxfords; Senior play—Rust and black taffeta."

Also, many dance cards and tiny envelopes with disintegrated blossoms inside. "Commencement night—A dozen American Beauties; Senior play—A dozen American Beauties; Baccalaureate Sermon—Corsage of lavender and sweet peas; Inaugural Ball— Sweet Pea corsage."

She had saved concert programs from the Over-holser Theater and the Fairgrounds Auditorium, which was also known as the Horse Barn. Oklahoma had only been a state twelve years, yet the greats came to perform. She saw David Warfield, Jascha Heifetz, Alma Gluck, Galli-Curci. These perform-ances stayed with her all her life and she spoke of them often. On all the programs, the dance cards, many flower envelopes, over and over all through her book, she had written one name, "Calvin."

Under "Gifts," she had listed: "Grandma and Grandpa Alberts— Ten dollar gold piece; Uncle Fred and Aunt Crystal—Pink satin lingerie; Aunt Bertha and Uncle Paul—Gown with crocheted yoke; Aunt Daisy and Uncle John—Two camisoles, pink and green." On a separate page is listed: "Complete set of Browning. Calvin Grinnell, Senior Class Presi-dent."

On the page "Class Officers," in fine, beautiful script is written:

Dear Pauline,
From out the few last, lingering days of
joy and tumult, of urgent duties and of parting
sorrows, rises in the moment of alluring calm,
a mist of faces, dearest of the dear. It is small,
this group of dearest faces, for it comes from
the memory of those few who are more
precious than all else. It may be strange to
some, but not to me, that, though there may
be others there, I cannot see but one, and
though I strive to see whose else may come,

*hers comes to make me happier than theirs
ever could. 'Tis thine, dear girl, and sweeter
face is in no boy's mist of faces. Bless thee
and all that's thine and peace be with you till
we meet again.*

Calvin Grinnell

In the same handwriting, on the last page, is written:

*The snow fell.
An old worn out discountenanced creature
plodded through the slush. In his eye was the
look of the wanderer, who ever seeks and
seeking never finds. Peace, no doubt, but he
cannot find it. Companions, but not for him.
The flower bloomed. A maiden as sweet and
fresh as the dew, which hesitates beneath the
morning sun, raised her head above the roses
to look upon the world. Pure were her
thoughts, inspiring all who knew them. She
was the true friend of real friends. They met,
these two, in the crowded street, on
humanities breakers, as it were. She smiled at
him; a beam of light that opened a door long
closed. Faltering, he stretched forth a hand;
straightening, she took it. Heaven and earth
were one.*

How could she resist him? This Calvin Grinnell, with the pen of a poet, this natural leader, with exceptional intellect and sensitivity. Reading what he

wrote, I almost fell in love with him. To overcome
him, Papa must have had something very powerful.
She may very well have been in love with Calvin
Grinnell. Her book certainly indicates she was, but
perhaps she sensed that despite all his sensitivity, she
was missing something in him. When she met Papa,
it woke a part of her that she had never felt with
Calvin. That strong attraction victimized her, as it
does all women, especially when it hits for the first
time. She tried to resist it their entire 63 years
together, and she was never out of the power of it.
Nor he with her.

Like a lot of scary bright people, she was an enig-
ma. She was impatient with those less intelligent,
high strung, easily irritated, often at the mercy of
her nerves; hence, "utterly exhausted, in a state of
nervous prostration." When telling a story or relat-
ing an event, she would urge the teller to "Get on
with the narrative. I'm five jumps ahead of you."

When she was reading, which she was during most
of her waking hours, if a child pestered her she would
slam the book shut and cry, "I have tried in vain to
read this paragraph five times! What do you want
NOW?" She munched Cheez-it crackers and drank
bottled RC Cola, which we were not allowed to have
because caffeine is bad for children. Of course this
did not prevent us from whining for just a sip or a
bite of whatever she was eating. Sometimes she'd
relent, saying, "If it was arsenic, you'd want it!"

She had little domestic sense and less interest.
She allowed Caroline, her first child, to cut her teeth

on her sterling silver candlesticks. She said she treasured them more with a baby's teeth marks.

She kept house as little as possible. Her silver was always black, her beautiful Oriental rugs often went unvacuumed for weeks, and her mahogany secretary was crammed with newspaper clippings (torn, never scissored), broken pencils, dried up pens and expired grocery coupons spilling out of used envelopes. Every glass door knob as well as her wrists were encircled with dozens of rubber bands, like some weird religious fetish.

She was of average height, small-boned, very pretty, with a lovely full bosom and a tiny waist. She also had tiny feet and hands, so small I couldn't get her rings on my little finger. When Papa ordered her wedding rings, the jeweler asked if he was marrying a child bride. She was refined, genteel, a lady who wore White Shoulders perfume, lovely hats, and always carried gloves and a linen handkerchief. However, there were days when she never dressed, she was so deeply engrossed in her reading. She often sat outside because, she said, "This house is such a mess, I couldn't stand it any longer, so I just had to come outside and read." If she was caught without a book, a sort of panic beset her and she became like a fussy child, restless and apprehensive. To ward this off until she got her book fix, she would conjugate Latin verbs and do mathematical equations. She was not content to know the answer, but wanted to know *why* it was the answer.

She was "pressured" into joining clubs, where she

was always elected president. She claimed, "You don't know how it bores me. These people drain my energies and give me no peace!" It was all a pose. She loved it; despite her proclaimed desire to be left alone, she was sociable, hung on the phone for hours, and had many friends. When questioned about this contradictory trait, she said, "You don't understand. I don't like people, but they interest me."

While she possessed unswerving concentration, she also was often distracted, forgetful and, a terrible procrastinator. At least twice a month, panic would hit the household because she had lost her wedding rings. All us children would fan out to search the house and yard. She would call Papa at his office, wild with anxiety, only to have him tell her, "Pewliny (Pauline), look in the ice box." They always turned up, usually buried in a broken sugar bowl where she had hidden them.

She was highly intuitive and had a keen insight into people's motivations and the hidden meaning behind their words. She was very suspicious and aware of the slightest signs of manipulation.

When she taught school, the school board broke her contract, claiming she was sick. She said she wasn't sick, but pregnant, and sued the school board for the remainder of her salary and won.

The minister once accused her of writing an anonymous letter, saying maybe she wanted to move her letter to another church. She wrote the preacher, "I have been a member of the First Presbyterian Church since before you were born. I was married there and all four of my children were baptized there. Only my death will cause my departure from this church, at which time it will be you who will be long gone to another church. I never signed anything anonymously in my life. I stand behind my beliefs. You not only have erred in your judgment of me, but you have misjudged the anonymous letter writer as well, not knowing him any better than you do me. You are a shepherd who does not know his flock!"

A woman named Alice Hughes, a syndicated newspaper columnist, once misquoted Browning, which Mama was quick to spot. She wrote her pointing out her error and advised her to check her references. Alice Hughes wrote back saying she was actually quoting Kirk Douglas, who had quoted Browning, and wasn't it a wonderful thing that someone coming from his background was familiar with Browning. Mama was not about to let her get by with that; she wrote back, "Your letter is condescending, and it is your name that is on the column, not Mr. Douglas'. I repeat — check your references. To misquote Browning is as inexcusable as misquoting Shakespeare, Milton or the Bible."

As a child, I longed for the aproned, domestic mothers of my friends. By junior high, I had begun to grasp how superior my mother was to that. As my friends were growing away from their mothers, I was beginning to appreciate mine—her depth, her complexity, her uniqueness, and her vision for me. Her primary interest was not our food, clothes, or physical well-being. She somehow counted on those things taking care of themselves. What consumed her above all else was the nurturing of our characters, the pursuit of our goals, the development of our abilities. She believed, like the ancients, that the purpose of life was not to be happy, but to matter, to have it make some difference that you lived at all, and that happiness in the ancient, noble verse means self-fulfillment and is given to those who use to the fullest whatever talents, fate, luck or God had bestowed upon them. She believed that we make our own luck, and that "Luck favors those who are prepared."

She insisted that we be responsible for our own actions, be disciplined, and stay focused. One of her friends once told her that if she was too harsh on her children they wouldn't love her. She responded, "It is not paramount that my children love me. What is first and foremost is that they be taught to be good citizens and contributing members of society. A parent has to be able to bear the anger of their children while they are disciplining them for their own good."

Her moral teachings were often expressed with literary quotes. "Truth crushed to earth will rise again." "He who would sacrifice essential freedom for temporary security deserves neither freedom or security." "Honor is hard to come by. And pride that flows from honor is not false." At one of my Fourth of July parties, she stood and recited a portion of the Declaration of Independence—from memory. She was 90 years old.

My entire life we were in constant correspondence. Thousands of letters passed between us, even when she was nearly blind with glaucoma, the most tragic disease that could befall a voracious reader. Her letters were almost illegible, but still they came, often marked "Postage Due." They were full of clippings, advice, and always encouragement. Typical was:

> Nothing in the world can take the place of PERSISTENCE.
>
> Talent will not; nothing is more common than unsuccessful men with talent.
>
> Genius will not; unrewarded genius is almost a proverb.
>
> PERSISTENCE and DETERMINATION alone are omnipotent.
>
> The slogan PRESS ON has solved and always will solve the problems of the human race.

She died surrounded by her children. Papa had given her a heavy, narrow Indian bracelet that she had not taken off in 70 years, not even when her children were born. The funeral home gave us a packet, and when we opened it, we were heartsick to see this silver bracelet. My sister said that when Papa saw her, he would say, "Why, Pewliny, girl, where's my bracelet?" So, before the funeral, her coffin was opened and she went to her grave wearing Papa's bracelet.

She was buried on my birthday. As I had come from her on that day, it was only fitting that I paid tribute to her leaving on that day. I ended my remarks with two of her favorite poems:

> Lives of great men all remind us
> We too should make our lives sublime
> And departing leave behind us
> Footprints in the sands of time."

And from her beloved Browning:

> One who never turned his back but marched
> breast forward,
> Never doubted clouds would break,
> Never dreamed, though right were worsted,
> wrong would triumph,
> Held we fall to rise, are baffled to fight better,
> Sleep to wake.

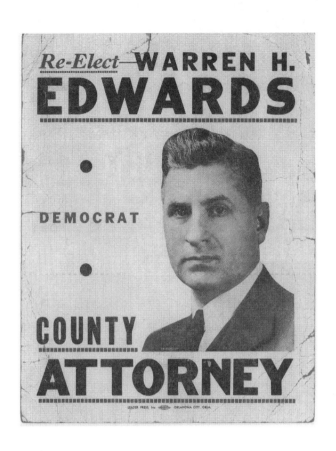

PAPA

Laid flat were campaign posters. Mama hated it when Papa entered politics. She said she agreed with Alexander Hamilton, who "wasn't much attached to the multitudes." She argued that being a public servant was just that, being on call for all the riffraff in the country.

As a kid, I loved it. Before television, campaigning was done with fliers, newspaper ads, posters with the candidates pictures stapled to telephone poles

and on wooden stakes in people's yards. If a neigh-
bor had a sign for a candidate that was different from
yours, there could be strained relations until after
the election.

Papa drove all over the county stump speaking in
an old-fashioned Model T Ford that he kept in beautiful condition. It was spiffy, black with silver lettering on its sides, "Warren H. Edwards, Democrat for
County Attorney."

We would canvas the neighborhoods, which meant
my brother and sisters and I would each be assigned
so many square blocks to knock on doors and hand
out little cards with Papa's picture and name on
them and say, "Please vote for my father Warren H.
Edwards for County Attorney." Some of these
neighborhoods were dangerous and seemed to be
filled with big black cur dogs and women, their hair
in pin curls, standing behind screen doors hollering,
"Blackie! Git back in here!" I developed a sympathy
for postmen.

I asked Papa what I should do if they said they
were voting for another candidate, and he said to be
courteous. I said that they were wrong and I wanted
to tell them off. Papa said, "Not wrong, just mis-
guided. Never bray at an ass."

We campaigned in Sandtown (a sink of crime), a
shantytown of tar paper shacks covered with corru-
gated tin and old license plates (down in the Canadi-
an River bottom). I loved it when we went into a
big wooden dance hall called Mulligan's Gardens.
There was a flame-haired woman who yodeled and

sang, "I Want To Be A Cowboy's Sweetheart." She wore a red satin shirt with fringe, a buckskin skirt with butterflies branded on it and a pair of go-to-hell boots. Many times a brawl would ensue and we'd have to get out of there fast.

Once, my older sister in enthusiastic loyalty and spirit of competition, tore Papa's opponent's signs off the telephone poles and proudly presented them to him. He took her to his opponent's headquarters, made her go inside and tell them what she had done and apologize. Then he drove her around town in the Model-T making her put them back up again.

The most fun were the rallies held in city parks at night when it was not so hot. There were always big crowds, sometimes a heckler or two, and lots of watermelon and soda pop. Papa was a wonderful speaker. In affluent neighborhoods he told them, "I'm not going to lie to you and tell you I was born out here in a dugout in Eastern Oklahoma. My father was a success and could afford to educate his children." In poorer areas, he'd say, "My people came to Oklahoma in a buckboard wagon. They knew what it was like to sleep under the wagon sheet." Both statements were true.

First there were the primaries, run-offs between Democratic candidates. Papa was a Jeffersonian Democrat. Whoever won opposed the Republican candidate, who never won. Mama's father was the only person we knew who voted the Republican ticket, but it was never discussed openly. Papa said it was because "Mr. Mills' father was a Yankee."

Election nights held a special excitement. It took time for the returns to come in which created enormous suspense. It was live, we were right there, part of an active election process. It was our election, individually.

Ballot boxes had a specific shape. We'd go down to the courthouse and watch padlocked, battered boxes coming in from precincts all over the county, hour after hour, heavily guarded. The atmosphere was always very serious, almost reverential. I asked Papa why and he said, "The People are speaking."

In another part of the courthouse, the votes would be tabulated and put on a blackboard. This was less serious, with shouts and groans, depending who you were for and how the precinct voted.

Papa carried every vote in his home precinct as well as his opponent's precinct. The newspaper had endorsed him enthusiastically. After he'd been in office about four months, the owner of the paper started telling Papa how he wanted things done. Papa told him to go to hell, he was no man's slave, that he'd been elected for the people, by the people to serve their interests and the dictates of his own conscience. He couldn't be bought, and that a man who would compromise his ethics may be walking around, but he's "dead as a beaver hat."

From then on it was war. Papa publicly called the editor "a tinhorn gambler and that lowdown bunch he's running with are scrub cattle." The editor wrote editorials denouncing Papa, and Papa lost the next election.

As I think back now, Papa was naive. He believed the paper had originally endorsed him because he was the best man for the job, not realizing that his very naiveté was what the editor was after. The editor thought he had a candidate he could control, but he was also naive. And ignorant. With Papa, he was barking up a cold trail.

Strange as it seems, it was hardest on Mama. It made her heartsick to see Papa hurt. But Papa took it well. He said, "If your old dog dies, you get a new dog. Onward and upward."

While he was still in office, Papa had been offered a large bribe. When she heard this, my grandmother said jokingly, "I always taught Warren to be honest. Sometimes I think I overdid it." When Mama heard this, she laughed so hard she stopped crying over Papa losing.

* * *

Papa believed and taught his children that a man's word was his bond and to always tell the truth because "Oh, what a tangled web we weave, when first we practice to deceive." He thought the only aristocracy was of the spirit and that you could judge a man by how he treated others. He said people revealed themselves by their behavior toward those who were less fortunate and that we must be good to all people, not just those who could do us a favor.

He worked the courtroom for 60 years. He could pull a quote for every occasion. Papa had to make those juries fall in love with him. He knew it was not just his client, but himself as well that was on trial. He had great personal charm and charisma. He was volatile, high tempered, eccentric, flamboyant, and possessed a shimmering wit. He was a vanishing breed with a rigid moral code, believing that compromise was the language of the devil. Most of his kind have died out, and the country is less because of it.

He was born in Wise County, Texas, and grew up in a time when gentlemen did not drink in front of ladies, so sometimes he'd go out behind the barn and take a pull of whiskey. He drank out of the bottle — like a preacher. He said he loved corn all the way from the cob to the bottle. He smelled of Jim Beam, Mail Pouch tobacco, saddle soap and bay rum. He loved horses, dogs, Texas, his family, his friends, and believed in the redemptive power of the land. He hated federal judges puffed up by their office and appointed for life. "Sucking off the public teat" is the way he described them. One of these judges once asked my father, "Mr. Edwards, are you showing contempt for this court?" Papa replied, "No, your honor, I'm trying to conceal it."

Between him and my mother ran an undercurrent of something nameless. They were married for 63 years. He said, "Thirty years ago I gave your mother a little silver bell. I told her to ring it if she ever had a pleasant thought. I've yet to hear it."

Often his clients couldn't pay him — in cash money, that is — so they gave him things. Anything from a grand piano with no ivories to a pregnant hunting dog, making the house resemble the last day of a large fire sale. For years we ate our cereal out of banana split dishes. We had 33 of them. It bothered Mama because it was a broken set. At one time, there were two grand pianos (out of tune, of course) in the living room, a pile of moth-eaten Oriental rugs in the dining room, and 22 cur pups out back.

It used to be said that Oklahomans would vote dry as long as they could stagger to the polls. Papa had befriended a bootlegger, LaRow Hare. He lived in one of those little shotgun houses you could sling a cat through. He had six kids with impetigo and four or five old turdhounds all covered in the mange.

To supplement his bootleg career, Mr. Hare was the head usher at the old Shrine Auditorium. Everything came there: the Ballet Russe de Monte Carlo, Don Cossack Chorus, Jose Iturbi, Tito Guizzare. Mr. Hare snuck us into all the performances free. No fee he could have paid Papa would have been so valuable. I always say I received my culturing from a bootlegger.

Papa wore a heavily starched white shirt, a deep red tie, a dark suit, his Masonic lapel pin, and a Waterbury watch with a winding key on a chain tucked in his vest pocket. He carried a large initialed linen handkerchief and wore a good Stetson.

When I was a kid, a treat was to help him take off his high-heeled boots. I'd straddle the boot backwards and grasp the heel while Papa pushed on my backside with his other foot and off would slip the boot. He designed his own boots and had them made in San Angelo, Texas where they'd had his mold for over 50 years. The tops were nearly to the knee with the Lone Star emblazoned on the sides. He wore those boots with tails when he escorted his daughters down the aisle of the First Presbyterian Church to be married.

He had inherited from his mother not only her talent for observation but her killing wit. Speaking of a brother-in-law, he once said, "He's got all the attributes of a dog, except loyalty." Speaking of another no-account, shiftless relative, my mother said, "Now, Warren, don't be so hard on him. He's improving." Papa replied, "Pauline, you can polish a rat's tooth for years and it'll never make ivory."

Sometimes I think it is a disadvantage to have had such a father because he is who you are always looking for. He was a hard act for any man to follow. Many of his ideas and convictions were not popular, but he didn't give a damn. He was who he was, said what he had to say, whenever and wherever he liked, without preface, fear, or apology. He knew who he was and had the courage to be true to it. As a consequence, those traits drew people to him, fascinated. He was deeply conservative, a keen observer of human nature and sympathetic to its frailties, generous to a fault, true to his friends.

He requested a Masonic funeral and we gave it to him. My brother designed and made the blanket that covered his coffin— magnolia leaves topped by white flowers in the shape of the Lone Star.

"Here's hoping that health is the horse under you
Ahead a long, easy ride
Good water and grass to the top of the pass
Where the trails cross the Big Divide."

BORN "ALIVE"

y birth certificate, I figured, had been lost for all time. I had been through every box, several times, shaken out the book pages, opened all the envelopes and checked the family Bible. Not a sign of it, so I hauled the box of baby didies and newspaper wrappings to the trash. When I dumped it into the garbage can, there was a mysterious thud. I retrieved what appeared to be four large, square parcels wrapped in crocheted baby blankets and tied with twine. I unwrapped them and saw they were scrapbooks, with a child's name on the front of each one. Inside were Father's Day and birthday cards that each child had sent Papa over the years. Over the next couple of days, I kept going through these scrapbooks thinking perhaps my birth certificate was hiding in plain sight. Finally, just when I had decided to put them away, I discovered two pages stuck together. When I pulled them apart, the construction paper broke off in pieces and inside was a bandana wrapped around an envelope on which was written, "Sophronia Gertrude Edwards." Inside, in Papa's handwriting, was a sheet of paper which read, "This child is as unruly as a Hessian. Before she lost her milk teeth, she was faunching at the bit and throwing a wall-eyed fit at every least little thing. Her tongue wags at both ends, mostly backtalk. She has inherited that Teutonic mule-headedness from her mother's people and I have not been able to breed it out. I pray to God the money I spent on getting her educated pays off. I have tried to teach her family pride and loyalty. I've told her repeatedly to stay out of the brush, keep her dress down, and ladies don't smoke. I believe she'd pull me out of the fire, but trying to corral her is like herding frogs."

I began to laugh, then cry, and ended up doing both. Papa would have called it, "The devil beating his wife," meaning rain was falling while the sun was shining. Laughter through the tears.

I replaced the letter. As I did so, I let out a holler; for there, in the same envelope, was a birth certificate. I actually hesitated before I opened it. Was I fearful to finally know who I was? Nervously, I unfolded it and read:

Oklahoma City Health Department.
Place of Birth: Oklahoma City, Oklahoma
Sex: Female
Legitimate: Yes
Father's Name: Warren Hamilton Edwards
Age: 33
Occupation: Attorney
Mother's Maiden Name: Pauline Caroline Mills
Age: 31
Number of children of this mother: 3
Signed by attending physician: Dr. E. Allen
Born: Alive
Date and time of birth: February 9. 12:03 a.m..
Full name of child: Not named Edwards."

Not named! Not named? How could this be? How could it have happened? Why had they never officially named me? Was it an oversight or was it done on purpose? But, for what purpose? What reason could possibly explain it? They were not careless people.

I had always known that I was a kaleidoscope of many people. Lionella, Miz Arnette, Uncle Homer, certainly my grandmother. I was a collage of their eccentricities plus some original ones thrown in. But this did not explain the mystery of "Not named" and what my parents' motivations were. I pondered over it for the next couple of months and it began to dawn on me that my thinking a name would help define me was all wrong. My parents believed it was character that defined a person, that life was a gift, and to be born was a privilege. Therefore, we had to give something back. "Don't just stand around and take up air." Being a good citizen was not enough. That was expected. We had to be contributing members of society. In so doing, it was not only society who benefited but ourselves as well, because it was personally rewarding. Work tells a person who they are, and there is no high like the joy of accomplishment. So they encouraged us to discover our talents, and then stay with it. Never, never give up because "Anyone can quit." Failure was accepted if you had tried, but no reason to stop trying. My folks believed in the Protestant ethic and that our choices on a daily basis added up to who we were. We could do anything we set out to do. The sky was the limit and nothing held us back but ourselves. There were no short cuts. It took tenacity, hard work, years of effort and commitment, but it could be done. Whatever we wanted was out there for us. This idea was so thrilling, exciting — the thought that our goal was just waiting for us individually. The future had our name on it, and it was a living, breathing, shining star beckoning to us, because "A man's reach should exceed his grasp, or what's a heaven for!"

I am beginning to accept that I will always be Not Named Edwards, because life is an ongoing accumulation of people and experiences. I am forever searching, changing, and finding on an endless quest. Because of these infinite and timeless journeys, I can never call, "Curtain. Finis. Exit. The End." Rather, I can only say, "To be continued . . .

June 12, 1980

Dearest Daughter Sophronia Gertrude,

I am longing to go to Texas. I need to see the Alamo once again before I die. Thermopylae had its messenger of defeat. The Alamo had none.

I send you my love, but not all of it because I have to save some for your brother and sisters.

I am, as ever, Your Paw,
W.H.E.